AN ANGLER'S GUIDE TO

BASS PATTERNS

Productive Methods, Places And Times

by Larry Larsen

Book VIII in the Bass Series Library
by Larsen's Outdoor Publishing

ISBN 0-936513-07-1

Library of Congress 89-92685

Published by:

LARSEN'S OUTDOOR PUBLISHING
2640 Elizabeth Place
Lakeland, FL 33813

First Edition

PRINTED IN THE UNITED STATES OF AMERICA

2

DEDICATION

To my brother, Ron Larsen, who shares a love of bass fishing and who has, over the years, added a sense of competitiveness to our on-the-water experiences. I have enjoyed studying the fish and keeping abreast of evolving techniques to catch more largemouth than Ron.

ACKNOWLEDGMENTS

I want to thank the newspaper and magazine reviewers of the previous books in my BASS SERIES LIBRARY for their kind comments. Outdoor writers like Frank Sargeant, Bob Bledsoe, Daryl Black, George Kramer, Ben Callaway, Bob Sarber, Dick Bowles, Bob Epstein, Bill McKeown, Larry Cribb, Louie Stout, Don Kirk, Mike Levy, Horace Carter, Bernie Keefer, Brian Sayner, Jim Brown, John Phillips, Del Milligan, Bill Sargent, Gordon Sprouse, Dan Cook, Bill Vanderford and Fred Bonner are a few of those that have spread the word on my books. There have been many more, and it would probably take several pages to list them all. I do appreciate all of them and their efforts. The outdoor writing community is a close-knit one, and I have many friends that travel in these same circles. With such support, the BASS SERIES LIBRARY will continue to provide additional reading for America's interested anglers.

The valuable review, layout and production assistance of my wife, Lilliam, is much appreciated. So is the input, over the years, of top magazine editors such as Bob Robb, Steve Pennaz, George Haas, Clare Conley, Spence Petros, Charlie Plueddeman, Keith Gardner, Biff Lampton, Robert Sloan, Jack Holmes, Mike Schwanz and Marvin Spivey. Again, there have been many others that also deserve thanks. The assistance of those professionals has helped me to become a professional outdoor writer. I appreciate that.

PREFACE

The "Angler's Guide To Bass Patterns" focuses, as the subtitle says, on productive methods, places and times. Being able to develop a pattern of successful methods and lures for specific habitats and environmental conditions is the key to catching several of them on one fishing trip. Understanding bass movements and activities and the most appropriate and effective techniques to employ will add many pounds of enjoyment to the sport of bass fishing.

"Bass Patterns" is a reference source for all anglers, regardless of where they live or their skill level. The book examines a variety of the most effective patterns, that combination of lure, method and places. The productive and proven techniques to catch both active and inactive bass are discussed. The reader should learn some interesting patterns that have not received much publicity. They are the most effective ones, under the right conditions, and this book carefully explains that relationship.

CONTENTS

ABOUT THE AUTHOR

For more than 18 years, Larry Larsen has studied and written about all aspects of bass fishing. His previously published books in the Bass Series Library detail highly productive fish catching methods and special techniques. He believes in explaining to readers the latest and very best tactics to find and catch bass anywhere.

Larry Larsen enjoys bass fishing as much as he enjoys writing about it. His angling adventures and research on the black bass have been extensive. He has caught and released numerous bass between five and 12 pounds and has literally traveled the globe to fish for largemouth and the uncommon species of bass. He has fished lakes from Canada to Honduras and from Cuba to Hawaii. He lives on Highland Hills Lake in Central Florida, where his bass boat sits at the dock.

The author is a frequent contributor to Outdoor Life, Sports Afield, Fishing Facts, and Field & Stream. More than 1,000 of Larsen's magazine articles have appeared in major outdoor magazines, including Bassin', North American Fisherman, Bass Fishing, and Petersen's Fishing. His photography has appeared on the covers of many national publications. Larsen is a member of the Outdoor Writers Association of America (OWAA), the Southeastern Outdoor Press Association (SEOPA), and the Florida Outdoor Writers Association (FOWA).

Larsen has now authored 8 books in the award-winning BASS SERIES LIBRARY, plus "Mastering Largemouth Bass", a 260-page hard cover book for the North American Fishing Club. Information on the author's BASS SERIES LIBRARY is available at the back of this book.

INTRODUCTION

LURE PERCEPTION

What Makes Bass Patternable?

A SIGNIFICANT KEY to patterning largemouth and then catching more of them is based upon an understanding of how they perceive the lure. Obviously, man can only make educated guesses on a lure's effect upon fish in a given environment. Color, shape and action seemingly have a lot to do with why a bass strikes a lure, and why others in similar habitat at that time may have a similar response.

Water clarity and depth and other environmental factors affect the predator's ability to perceive a lure as a food item. Forage availability and awareness also appear to greatly influence that perception. How a fake item is presented under those circumstances and its repeatability also enters into the activity pattern equation.

The speed of the lure determines whether you are employing a striking presentation or a feeding presentation. The faster the retrieve, the more likely a bass will strike out of reflex action. In dirty water, fish can't see the lure as well. They generally won't have time to smell a quick-moving bait, so an angler may have just reduced the impact on three of the fish's senses. It'll have to operate only on hearing and vibrations.

Bass will move up maybe 20 feet after a noisy surface lure, like a buzz bait. They can hear the vibration that the lure gives off from a tremendous distance. Bass will come much further after a buzz bait than they will a spinnerbait. That's particularly true in deeper off-color water, because a buzz bait gives off a lot more vibrations.

Bass have a tremendous appetite, but some studies have shown that they tend to have a forage type preference. They like a long thin

Once an effective pattern is established, several bass can be caught. For bass tournament professionals, like Jimmy Houston, that means culling the smaller largemouth will be possible.

prey better than they do a short, fat one, and they're basically efficiency-oriented as is any predator. That appears to be a natural course of evolution. Bass are able to swallow a long and heavy baitfish easier than they can a short and heavy one.

The short, fat baitfish that stay in the weeds tend to adapt to the color of the weeds. They usually have the bar/stripe pattern and spines. They generally are more solitary than are shad, for example, which roam the open waters. Forage like sunfish and bluegill don't rely on speed to outrun a predator, but they can move very quickly into the weeds.

Generally, a lure that appears natural and mimics forage will increase its productivity. In some instances, though, an exact replica could be a disadvantage because some colors can be protective measures. Colorations such as a vertical yellow and black stripe may tend to discourage predation and not trigger hunger or excitement.

One of the most common defense mechanisms on baitfish is the false eye. It's a focal point that's usually toward the back to draw the predator's strike. It may be much bigger than the real eye on the head and look like a big pupil. On some baitfish, it may even be ringed in a color, such as orange, like the iris. In nature, the predator is so distracted by the "false eye" that he will often strike the tail. Thus, lures that emphasize the forage triggers, like a big eye, can be very productive.

A sense of direction may be what a predator looks for when he follows the prey; he looks for the front or lead before he strikes. An angler may be helping him out by putting a big eye on the lure, and making it easier for the predator to find that head part. That's one way, some believe, to turn the color defense mechanism around and make the lure more vulnerable.

Based on the disadvantages and advantages of color versus black and white vision, most experts believe that bass would not have adapted to color vision unless they need to see in the day in order to feed. Catch records of many big bass experts prove it. They catch most of their fish in the high-sun times of day.

Solar Fish

I constantly watch fish in the lake behind my house. They stay right up close to the surface when the sun shines. Even right through the middle of the day, when I walk to the bank, I can see boils on the surface where the fish are suspended with their backs almost out of the water up in the sun. Sunlight is vital to their metabolism, since bass are a sunfish.

One of the ways to have an advantage over their prey is for the bass to keep their body temperature up. Cold weather creatures' metabolism is elevated and their senses are keener if they're warmer. The colder they are, the slower they get. Bass are similar to snakes in that they sometimes soak up sun before they feed in order to warm up their body temperature. If the fish can keep a little bit warmer than the prey, he has some advantage when motivated to strike for hunger reasons.

FIGURE 1 - An angler can get a little extra edge by appealing to the fish's sense of smell and taste. Some baits, like Berkley's Power Worms, are fortified with scent and flavor enhancers.

Big bass will eat most in the summer, every two or three days, and that's when they are easiest to pattern. A lot of bass can eat five or six shad and shiners at once, given the opportunity. At other times, they will barely be able to feed on that much over the course of a week. That's when getting them to strike a lure can be particularly difficult. An angler may generate follows but no "takers."

Once bass are in the immediate proximity to the lure, then the key to motivating them to strike may be in appealing to their other senses. Scent and odors are close-range things that fool fish into believing that the lure is forage. They don't work on bass from a long distance, but they can provide an extra incentive for a nearby fish to eat the bait.

An angler can get a little extra edge by appealing to the fish's sense of smell and taste. Although bass use their sense of sight similar to the way humans do, they are much better than us at utilizing their other senses. Smell has two components to the fish:

positive and negative. When the bass are aggressive, you may catch fish almost regardless of odor, but when they are sluggish, you need to be careful about smell and taste. Scent leaves an odor track that the fish will pick up, and reinforces the visual attraction.

Book Patterns

How largemouth perceive any lure will always be a matter of opinion, but lure color, shape and action seemingly have influences. Why a bass strikes a lure depends on its mood and upon several of the factors that we've defined. Being able to develop a productive pattern will result from the understanding of such and the implementation when appropriate.

"Angler's Guide To Bass Patterns" has been written as an informational guide for those with a basic understanding of the bass/forage relationship and the underwater environment. It is a guide to numerous productive patterns that one might find over the course of several days on the water. The book details the optimal patterns for specific habitat and environmental conditions that may exist.

Understanding the most appropriate lures, methods and times for a particular place is the focus of the book. Boat positioning, new water strategies and deep water concepts are presented in the three initial chapters. The variety of vegetation and the most common patterns are discussed in Chapters 4 through 6. Effective bass-catching patterns for wood, in the form of brush and docks, are explained in Chapters 7 and 8, while the following chapter presents best tactics for rock habitat.

In Chapters 10 and 11, productive moving water patterns are discussed, and then, effective techniques for open water and windy waters are presented. The final chapters, 14 and 15, detail those patterns that are often the most difficult to establish, those for inactive bass, those in seasonal transitions and those suspended off-structure. As you wade through the chapters, try to recall experiences of your own that confirm these productive patterns. If you don't have several "confirmations," they go out and try them. That's the fun part!

CHAPTER 1

BOAT POSITIONING

Lure Presentations Depend On It

ONE OF THE MOST critical parts of establishing a productive pattern is often overlooked by many. Boat positioning can mean the difference between a nice catch of fish and no catch at all. It is not just new boat owners that make big mistakes by not understanding the importance of boat control. It's those that have been fishing a lifetime also.

Anglers run their rigs into boat docks, timber and other emergent obstructions frequently on many lakes, and usually, anytime you bump the cover, especially with shallow fish, you will spook them. Boat control is very critical to certain techniques, but it is also vital to almost any technique regardless of the cover. For example, I've vertical-jigged a lead spoon above submerged hilltops on deep reservoirs in Texas and the lure position has to be very precise there. The colder it is, the more precise the placement of a jigging spoon must be to produce.

In general, when working a submerged hump, you should position the boat in deeper water and approach the shallower top of the hump. That will normally prevent spooking the fish lying on top. When vertically working the hump with a jigging spoon or jig and eel, start at the top and work down the slopes until contact is made. A good LCD or chart recorder will usually pinpoint the location of the fish.

Regardless of whether you use a foot or hand-control electric, when you touch the on-off button in shallower water (less than 10 feet deep), you have to be aware of the direction of thrust. The

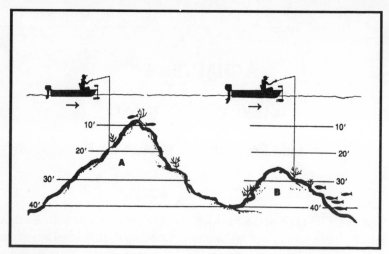

FIGURE 2 - Approach shallower cresting humps from the deep water so as not to spook the bass (A). Fish deeper humps from the top of the hump down the slope until fish contact is made (B).

electric motor that moves the boat to position an angler over a honey hole should become an extension of your legs or hands. After a while, using a trolling motor to set up you lure presentation will be as easy as walking. When you don't even think about directions as you hit the on-off switch, you have enough experience to correctly control the boat.

Many anglers make a big mistake by getting in a hurry and running the trolling motor on too high a speed. They come in on the cover too fast and end up reversing the direction. Then, they're blowing pressure waves back at the fish while trying to stop the forward momentum of the boat. While some smaller fish may not be affected, the bigger fish are extremely sensitive to that type of commotion.

The best way to operate the boat as you approach a target area is to work into the wind. Then when you do catch a fish and get off the trolling motor, you won't drift into or over the fish. The smart anglers will drift away from them which allows them to control everything. The angler won't drift in on the fish too fast because the wind is not controlling the boat's movement.

When fish are tight to emergent vegetation, it is usually best to move your boat near the cover and cast parallel to the weed edge. The author has found that proper boat positioning is the key to catching bigger bass.

Speed Of Approach

I use every speed on my trolling motor, depending on the wind, current and cover that I'm fishing, its density and the patterns that may be effective. I may run on the high 24-volt power all day long; and on other days, I'll set the speed extremely slow on 12-volt. When working very shallow water (as I often do) in a small area with a slow-type bait like a plastic worm, I may have the trolling motor set on "low 24".

There has been a lot of discussion about whether it's advisable to turn the trolling motor on and off a lot. I am in agreement with those that say either leave it on or off; don't turn the switch on and off constantly. I'll usually find a speed that is consistent with the cover that I'm fishing so that I can work it thoroughly.

The best way to cover an entire area thoroughly is to slowly move along and keep running the motor, rather than stop and go, stop and go. Most guides and professional anglers agree that the stop and go can be a turnoff for fish. Those that have observed underwater how fish relate to the sounds and vibration of the on and off switch feel that minimal usage is best.

To effectively fish any area, the key factors are selecting the right speed and how you approach the cover. When you are trying to cover a lot of water and develop patterns or pinpoint general areas to fish later, most of the better anglers run on higher trolling motor speeds.

When they don't need to cover as much water as possible and want, instead, to catch a bunch of fish from a specific structure, they'll slow down the approach. If the angler is new to the water and wants simply to look at a lot of cover and just catch a few fish to determine the active areas, then he should run on high speed and use fast-retrieve lures. Once you have found some fish, then you will want to slow down to work the cover or structure more thoroughly.

Gale Positioning

High winds blow many anglers "off the lake," or at least, to protected shores, and boat control is critical then for success. Under such conditions, prime fishing areas are generally along windward points and irregular shorelines. Both pose additional problems to the angler, but the catch can be improved substantially by correct boat control.

Dislodged plankton and small crustacean are suspended in the roily waters, attracting small forage fish. Larger predators know the conditions well and show up for the feast. Wind-blown, turbid waters and actively feeding bass make for greater success if the angler can fish the better areas.

I recommend four steps to more effectively catch bass under such conditions:

1. Lower the bow-mounted trolling motor to its maximum extension (depth) to minimize the time that the prop will be out of the water when the bow is forced up by the high waves.

2. Put the control on 24 volts and a low setting to maintain constant operation quartering into the wind. If you need additional instantaneous power, you only need to "throttle up;" you are already in the 24-volt mode, and that's the key. The boat will be under

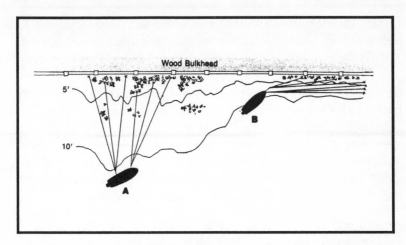

FIGURE 3 - If the depth beside the bulkhead or bank is shallow with vegetation, position the boat for casting perpendicular to the cover (A). If the bottom drops off quickly near shore, position the boat so that you and your partner can cast parallel to the cover from the bow (B).

maximum control when you are under continuous power.

3. Use the foot control from a seated position. You need maximum control of the operation and it is all but impossible from a standing position in high seas.

4. I throw a fast-moving bait such as a crankbait or spinnerbait. The bass are active, the boat is moving and there is no time or need for a "finesse" bait.

Even in the roughest weather, following these steps will maximize your chances of filling your livewell.

When Close Counts

At times, you can get extremely close to bass without spooking them with the trolling motor. I'll never forget working along a 15-foot wide river and catching bass after bass from right next to the bow-mounted electric. They were holding in brush and dense bulrushes and didn't seem to mind the intrusion of the electric.

I had thought initially that I was in too close on the first fishy-looking habitat, an old cypress stump at the edge of the creek. My boat's bow had been pushed toward it by the current and had the trolling motor turned around. You could see some of the silt and debris blowing out underneath the stump on the downstream side.

My plastic worm, rigged Texas-style, fell down beside the stump, and even with all the commotion from the trolling motor prop, a three pounder grabbed the bait. That largemouth bass couldn't have been two foot from the head of the trolling motor when he grabbed that lure. The stained water was blowing right into his face.

I caught and released about 15 bass up to 4 1/2 pounds that sunny morning from that creek. The current was significant and probably aided my slow and precise movements. It could have helped mask the boat's approach and noise of the electric motor.

Noise Controls

Living in Florida, I often have an opportunity to fish shallow water. In such an environment, a quiet motor is critical. You can't afford to spook fish.

In the old days, the early trolling motor props would hit the bottom and the baitfish would scatter across the surface. When that happened, I just have to assume that any bass there also got spooked. With many of today's trolling motors, we don't see that as often.

Noise turn-offs to fish are not only from the sound of the motor. A loose motor bracket that clangs every time you hit the bottom may spook fish. An abused prop with numerous burrs and nicks will put out additional pressure waves, possibly scaring off fish. Those are things that the angler can and should control.

You need to be aware of the noise that the trolling motor makes. Just like any piece of equipment, you have to maintain it. There may be bolts that need to be tightened or other things that need to be taken care of. When you use the equipment as much as most avid anglers do, its condition is critical to angling success.

Controlling The Fish

Another important consideration in boat control comes into play when the bass has struck the bait. You have to be very aware of where the fish is in relation to the trolling motor. If the fish makes a run toward the shaft, you may need to maneuver your rod to prevent an entanglement.

Large bass are most easily spooked by improper boat positioning and electric motor use. The first few casts should be parallel to the weed edge.

The first thing you must do is gain control of the fish with your rod. As long as he's moving away from you, the trolling motor and outboard can be cleared. On those occasions when you have hooked a big fish in open water, you may be able to reach down and raise the electric motor from the water to make sure that it is out of the way.

You could then trim up the outboard engine to prevent any potential problems at the rear of the boat. A great place to place a trim button is near the bow casting platform. If you have such, you can easily hit the switch with your toe to raise the rear engine.

Where the trolling motor is mounted for best, efficient use should be determined by the individual. Anglers that are left handed sometimes mount their electric motor on the right side. One consideration is that it be mounted so that the angler can make a cast and put the trolling motor down at the same time. Likewise, being able to fight a big fish and pull the electric motor up, if needed, is a real advantage.

This is most advantageous for a fishermen wanting to make every cast count. The placement and handling of the trolling motor may make a difference of only 50 casts over a day, but that could mean the difference between two bass and four.

Height Adjustments

I prefer my trolling motor positioned fairly high in the water. There is no need to have the bow-mounted electric positioned all the way down if you are fishing in three feet of water. Some of the "recommendations" that I would make are:

1. The prop should not break the surface, but in shallow water a raised shaft and prop keeps me from hitting many a stump and possibly bending the shaft.

2. When fishing structure in rough water with large waves are pushing at you, the prop shouldn't come out of the water every few seconds when the bow of the boat comes up. You can drop the motor back down some then. It's adjustable, so that you can adapt it to the conditions as they change.

3. Pay careful attention to the trolling motor prop, and, if conditions warrant, quickly change it. When the vegetation is so

heavy that you have to constantly pull up the motor and clean the prop, then go to a weedless prop to penetrate the cover.

Most companies today have a motor designed for a weedless prop that will handle any kind of vegetation. In some cases, though, the angler may be wise to go back to the regular props, when he doesn't need the weedless feature. They are often quieter and probably have a little more thrust.

Most anglers believe that the more fish are pressured, the more accustomed they get to trolling motor sounds. Fish that are accustomed to the sounds probably aren't scared but are put on alert. At other times, the bass may not even know what the trolling motor noise is. It varies from water to water.

I prefer to use a foot control model on my boat's bow because I don't want any wasted movement. Many anglers today like a hand-operated model, but I feel that they are at a disadvantage. Motors manufactured today are made so that you no longer have to worry about the foot-control cable breaking.

A lot of people began using the hand-controls because they thought that they would hold up better under all conditions. To that end, some anglers even carry an additional trolling motor in their rod locker just for insurance. Seldom will they ever need it. Equipment is built for durability these days.

The approach is often the key to catching bass. Successful anglers' accomplishments usually reflect how the careful and planned approach works.

CHAPTER 2

NEW-WATER STRATEGIES

Habitat And Lure Selections

THE WORD IS...that poachers have been arrested with some healthy fish from those waters. The lake has been sitting there, off-limits to anglers, for over three years, and big bass are swimming all over this impoundment.

You'll have a legal chance at catching a bunch when the lake officially opens. When that day arrives, naturally a lot of fish are taken. Many anglers find multitudes of small bass, but several are disappointed with their take of bass from the 'red hot' waters.

What happened? Why were just a few of the initial contingent of anglers successful at catching some heavy fish? Don't chalk the rewards up to luck. Those anglers simply addressed the unique situation posed by a newly-opened impoundment and quickly solved some of its mysteries.

Sure, a lake without any fishing pressure will support a cooperative bass population, and there are usually several of those waters around the country. When opened, most anglers will be able to catch several bass. Those who are successful on trophy fish and find plenty of action (40 or 50 bass caught and released) will have established patterns for catching largemouth from the unique water.

I have fished several newly-opened lakes over the years. Several years ago, I fished Lake Texana as it filled and inundated lushly-vegetated terrain. The waters were typical of new Texas reservoirs that seem to pop up almost each year. When I first visited the lake, the impoundment was in its infancy and stood at about half of its full flood pool watershed of 12,000 acres.

Heavyweight bass frequent the points in most waters, particularly those receiving little fishing pressure. When waters are opened to public angling, develop a quick pattern to get in on more than your share of big bass.

Finding points of access on a lake that is only half full is difficult, but my partner and I found an old inundated roadbed that served the launch purpose. My boat was the only one on the lake as I motored up the reservoir to look it over. Although others had been there before us, I felt that the tough launching conditions and very limited access to that point had made us pioneers on a new frontier.

The bass evidently hadn't felt the presence of many anglers prior to that day, for our results were fantastic. From our first stop at the nearest treeline and my first two casts, the bass simply could not resist our offerings. We didn't exactly catch a fish with every cast, nor were our results even close to that kind of efficiency, but we did catch and release well over 120 bass in about four hours of fishing.

The feisty bass concentrations were not in the submerged, heavily-wooded forests that were abundant around the lake. We found most of the big schools to be on the tapered, shallow flats, the ones with dense grass in about three or four feet of water. The rounded points on the windward shores were the most productive.

The wind would push the tiny, one-inch-long shad into the weedy point, where the bass would lie in wait. The most effective lure for the average 12-inch largemouth proved to be the mini crankbaits, three-quarters to one-inch long. When tossing the tiny baitfish replicas to the schools, my partner and I 'doubled' many times, and I even had a double catch on my plug.

I returned the following day and again caught well over 100 bass in four hours of pleasurable angling. All the bass were released to grow. Several were smaller than 12 inches and a few were as long as 17 inches. The larger ones were undoubtedly native northern largemouth bass which existed in the river, and in the small stock tanks which were inundated by reservoir waters as they slowly filled the lake. This is fairly typical of newly-impounded waters.

Regulating New Waters

Reservoirs like that produce some larger bass if the fish existed in the river prior to the damming. Most of the new impoundments in southern states are stocked with Florida-strain largemouth fingerlings. They are often placed in small ponds that exist along a watershed, prior to their inundation. As the water levels encroach, the retaining structures are then cut through, allowing the more-established bass total access to reservoir waters.

Forage is also often stocked heavily in new impoundments, and threadfin shad are ideal for such introductions in the South. The success of the bass fishery often parallels the 'blooming' of the shad population. The largemouth from such forage-intensive waters are normally fat and healthy, and without exception, full of flight.

The bass usually feel a compulsion to do acrobatics top side where the air medium does not impede their energetic maneuvers. Call it 'getting to know their adversary' or whatever, but they often take flight to look over the new situation they find themselves in.

Fishing 'new' water with lush, submerged vegetation and lots of fat healthy bass is a unique experience. The different types and colors of plants and weeds which abound pose new targets for the angler to aim his cast, and excellent cover for the quarry. The first three or four years' growth on a new impoundment typically cause the bass population to explode. New impoundment largemouth

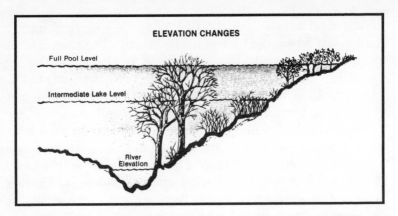

ELEVATION CHANGES

Full Pool Level

Intermediate Lake Level

River Elevation

FIGURE 4 - As a newly impounded lake rises, various types of vegetation are covered with water. Hardwood trees near the old river bed may be good early in the impoundment's life, but their value will usually decrease as a warm-weather hot-spot as waters rise. Scrub-type trees, then denser brush are next covered with water and become hot fishing areas. As waters clear after a few years and finer wood begins to rot, the fish will tend to drop back to deeper structure and edges.

often grow several inches in year one, and should be pushing 17 or 18 inches in a few years.

Several additional characteristics make for great bass fishing in new impoundments: good water quality, wind-blocking shoreline, irregular shoreline, moderately stained water color, numerous shallows and vegetation and deep structure.

Most new reservoirs are partially cleared, providing trollers unencumbered access; however, many trees are normally left along the submerged river bed and in some coves. Convenient boat lanes leading behind flooded tree wind blocks are often found on new impoundments. Open areas nestled between those forests and hilltop shores provide sheltered fishing areas away from wind, water skiers and speedboaters.

Fish shelters in the form of artificial reefs constructed of thousands of tires are often installed in new impoundments to enhance the structure. The new reefs are often placed prior to the lake's filling, and are usually marked with the appropriate fish attractor buoy. Tire reefs can be positioned along convenient bass migration routes.

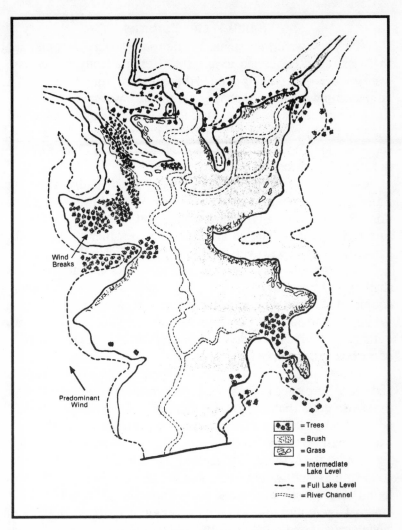

Legend:
- = Trees
- = Brush
- = Grass
— = Intermediate Lake Level
---- = Full Lake Level
::::::: = River Channel

Wind Breaks

Predominant Wind

FIGURE 5 - Bass populations in new impoundments will literally explode the first few years. These newly-created waters generally have excellent water color and fertility, plenty of cover-coated shallows, an abundance of forage and roaming fish that have not yet adapted to hard-to-fish spots. Lush vegetation forms wind breaks to aid anglers on windy days, a feature not found on most older reservoirs.

Small Water Patterns

Many new waters are small. I visited a 2,000-acre impoundment that was recently opened to anglers. Reports from the reservoir were good, and bass limits of up to three pounds were common. The largemouth were in good shape, and the lake was new.

Actually, the area had existed for several years. Creek waters allowed the impoundment to be flooded with waters containing small bass and food fish. Supplemental stockings of Florida bass set the stage for a prospering fishery.

One end of the reservoir was pretty much undisturbed. Its shoreline and numerous island banks were overgrown with vegetation. Weeds and small trees were abundant and emerged from the surface in all shallow areas. The islands on the other end were fairly barren, and there was evidence of recent digging in that area.

The reservoir was deep, dropping to 38 feet in some spots, but shallows did exist. In fact, most of my bass in two trips came from a couple of shallow sloughs in the older part of the impoundment. While my partner and I caught over 100 largemouth on the two outings, they were not everywhere, nor were they easy to find by the other boats that worked the lake.

My first time on this reservoir was spent with a lake veteran - he had been there once before. We tossed crankbaits and worms along the dense grass that hugged the shoreline of the older part of the lake. I had picked up six bass and my partner two from the steep banks when we boated to the mouth of a cut into a shallow slough.

"Let's try it in there," I suggested. He remarked that it sounded good to him, and we entered some of the best fishing that I have found. Our plastic worms and rubber crayfish were gobbled up by hungry largemouth. We left the high-noon findings one hour later, having caught and released around 40 bass.

Forage was as abundant as the vegetation in the slough, and the largemouth bass ranging from one to 5 1/2 pounds were numerous. The second trip further verified the lush vegetation/new waters pattern. A friend and I each took over 30 bass in about two hours from the area. A check-out of the less dense cover on newly excavated portion and of the deeper haunts in both sections resulted in very little for two additional hours of effort.

As reservoirs are dammed off and begin filling to capacity, lush green vegetation is inundated by the rising water. Knowing where to fish in an area full of "bassy-looking" spots is extremely important. Not all flooded terrain holds fish.

Approaching New Waters

Each year, plenty of 'new' waters with approachable largemouth are opened to public fishing. A plan of action on them is important to an angler's success, and certain pieces of information are vital to developing a sound strategy of attack. Things like depth variation, pH levels, cover available, water clarity and color and angling pressure can be determined while 'on the water.'

Other information of value might be checked out ahead of time by querying the right agencies. Such facts are the stocking and fishery management program, the source of run-in water, soil types and variation, availability of public access, size, extent of clear cutting prior to impoundment, and fish population breakdown. These factors will improve the angler's ability to find the best pattern.

The most important aspect of a new lake is that of the predator/forage relationship. Knowing the predominant prey of the bass will enhance the angler's lure selection and his success. Pertinent information can be obtained through a quick stomach analysis, or by observation of activity in the shallows. I've always felt that being familiar with the forage base (population breakdown and average size) will aid an angler in establishing a productive pattern quicker.

Maps generally aren't available for newly-opened waters, so you'll have to survey the potential bass haunts yourself. A good LCD or chart recorder is of great value on new, unmapped waters, both for navigation and for finding fish. Ride the lake and get to know it. Make sketches. Eliminate those areas in the reservoir that do not have the fish production potential.

Deep, rocky areas with clear water should be passed on by. Snag-infested spots, on the other hand, should be remembered and ultimately fished. Deeper structure and breaks are important, if consistent with the cover provided in shallower waters. Check out interesting structure thoroughly. Chart it and then fish it. Try to develop a pattern with it.

The shoreline can often be interpreted to give you an idea of the nearby structure and depth changes. Shallow waters do not generally abut steep rocky shores. Read the shorelines and watch for changes in soil characteristics.

Points of sand, gravel or stone are often good spring bass spots. Steep banks of clay or rock can produce great fishing in the winter when fronts often move through quickly. Bass need to be near deep water for their retreat until the cold snap passes. Tributaries are productive during spring and summer activity.

Shallow weedy spots, as mentioned, are bass 'hotels.' They are particularly packed in the spring but hold largemouth year around. A creek entering the cove adds to its magnetism. Bass will lie in such depressions awaiting a forage-ambush. The live bushes will attract the food chain and provide the adequate protection that a bass demands. Secluded flats and tapering points with substantial vegetation are hard to top.

Summer brings quick growing aquatic forms of vegetation, coontail, bulrushes and the like. These areas generally harbor concentra-

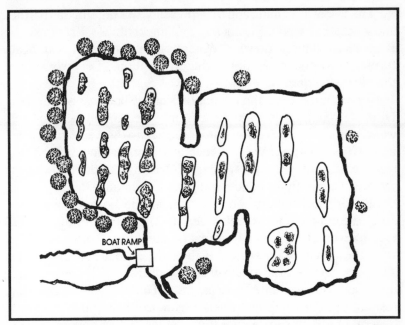

FIGURE 6 - Man-dug waters can be open in phases, and usually the more over-grown are the better bass grounds. Bass seek cover in all waters because it reveals fertility and correspondingly, forage.

tions of bass during the fall. Aquatic life, such as insects and other small organisms, starts the process. Anglers tossing weedless lures to the appropriate spots complete it.

While the other anglers are nonchalantly working every inch of a new impoundment and catching an occasional fish, you can be throwing back five times the bass they are catching. The lunkers will end up on your line, with a sound strategy.

Deeper Structures

Bass on recently-opened reservoir aren't always in shallow, vegetated areas. I fished a body of water which had been in existence for ten years or so, yet was off limits to fishing, until that opening day. Floating vegetation was clogging many small coves and bays in the lake. Flooded brush, cattails, bulrushes and hydrilla made the aquascape a fishery paradise.

Shad were abundant, and their presence was noted as my partner and I motored into a productive-looking spot. As I shut off the Evinrude, I glanced down. "Water color is wrong," I said, again turning the outboard ignition to the 'on' position. "Let's work out of this chalky-colored water."

Two minutes later, the visibility beside the boat was a clear stain. I shut off the engine and we began fishing. We worked the weed line, which was in about 15 feet of water. We cast to the stick-ups in three to seven feet of water. We took several bass on plastic worms and top water baits, but not until we began charting the depths with my recorder did we find a concentration of largemouth.

Bass concentrations were lying near the bottom on shelves ranging from eight to 12 feet in depth. The adjacent water was 20 feet deep on one side and four feet on the other. The bass schools would lie in wait for shad to wander by and then feed heavily on them. The bass were suckers for silver shad replicas.

Crankbaits accounted for a majority of our three hours of action, resulting in the catch and release of more than 100 largemouth. Several of the bass were over four pounds and had probably been there for years, undisturbed by anglers.

Activity of any kind on this reservoir was nil. Anglers pounding the shoreline of the newly-opened water found perhaps six or eight bass, the largest of which might have pushed the scales to three pounds. Bigger "school" fish were present on the deeper structure, however, and they were very approachable.

CHAPTER 3

DEEP WATER CONCEPTS

Getting Down For Frontal Bass

A BRUTAL COLD front is often something that most fish cannot escape. It is generally considered the most negative factor affecting transitional periods such as fall to winter or winter to spring. The influences of frontal conditions tend to dictate bass behavior to a certain point.

Several things happen in the aquatic environment as a result of cold fronts that we humans do not perceive. Before we draw any kind of reasonable supposition on why a front turns the fish off, we should understand the physical facts.

Bass generally react to a cold front by retreating into heavy cover, or they may get right down on the bottom and sit there. Scuba divers have often reported being able to swim very near fish in these circumstances without the fish swimming away. If bass swim away, they'll just circle behind the diver and move back to where they were.

"Bass react to their natural environment or surroundings," explains professional angler, O.T. Fears. "When a cold front comes through, the barometric pressure drops suddenly and then usually climbs up higher than it had been for several days preceding the front. Water temperature will cool a degree or two, depending on the severity of the front, the time of the year and where the lake is located geographically."

"In the midwestern states, a wintertime cold front won't affect bass depth too much," says Fears. "They are set in their winter depths and will not move much. The front will not affect the deep water temperature to a great degree."

Bass move deep seeking a comfort zone as winter sets in and continues. Stable cold weather during the winter will find bass positioned at that comfort zone, assuming that the oxygen and pH content of those waters are also "comfortable."

The surface temperature may change some, but the depths won't vary by more than a degree or two when a front pushes through, according to the former fishery biologist from Sallisaw, Oklahoma. Although the bass won't change their locations, they will change their feeding habits and their aggressiveness.

Cloudy skies during winter weather generally result in good fish catching opportunities, but after a strong cold front goes through, the fishing may be almost impossible. Bass will usually be inactive and bunched up in little depressions. If you go down a riverbank, they'll often be in an outside bend where it's deeper and usually offers jammed cover.

There won't be any fish cruising the banks where you might normally see them feeding, and where you might catch them. They would be so far back under any cover that you couldn't catch them. They're moody, too, because there are so many of them, and they're not used to competing with such a large group for limited forage. When you get too many fish in an area, particularly around spawning time, they'll often shut down and stop feeding.

Pre-spawn bass may be in relatively shallow water, 4 or 5 feet, so when a front hits, they may back off to 8 feet or so. If they are at a staging area, getting ready to spawn, they may just pull out into the middle of a cove. That's especially true if the cove is full of stumps.

Frontal Closeness

The front will usually cause the bass to move very tight to any structure. Stumps are some of the easiest structure to fish and they hold bass. Brush piles, though, are probably some of the most productive structures to fish then. Bass are harder to catch from them, because they are buried in the limbs, but they can be full of fish.

With the typical front, the humidity drops considerably. When it does, there are no clouds in the sky to scatter or filter out the blue light waves, or the ultraviolet spectra. As a result, the sky turns a pale, almost white blue after a cold front, and there's considerably more ultraviolet radiation reaching the water.

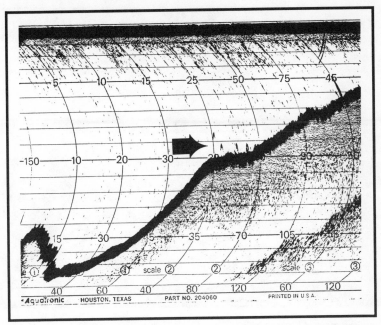

FIGURE 7 - You have to get right on top of bass and slow down a vertically-fished lure to catch fish after the front. These four are off of the bottom a few feet and catchable.

Bass have to go to the depths or get under something to replace the protection they normally get from clouds and humidity. Cumulus clouds and puffy, clear-weather clouds bring humidity, and that moisture scatters light. If the humidity decreases from 70% to 15% through 12 miles of atmosphere, it has taken a lot of water off. In effect, there's water over those fish before you even get to the lake.

Bass will often inhabit deeper parts, making fishing even tougher. In a shallow lake or river system, anglers can usually catch fish during a cold front because they find a concentration under heavy cover. In a deep reservoir, however, fish go deep when a cold front hits. Fears suggests smaller lures and lighter line after a front has passed.

"You have to get right on top of bass and slow down the lure presentation then to catch fish," he says.

"If the water is extremely clear, the cold front seems to affect the bass much more that in dingy water, where you may just be able to see

Smaller lures and lighter line fished on slopes are most effective, but first you have to use sonar and pH metering equipment to locate such structure with active bass.

a foot or two," Fears points out. "That has to do mostly with light penetration. The higher the barometer, the more light penetration you usually have in clear water."

Cold front bass seem to react to the light penetration in the water, and high skies with no clouds enhance such. As a result, the bass are more visible to their prey after the front, and they won't maintain an aggressive posture. They retreat further back from the perimeters of structure.

Water Chemistry Effects

"The amount of sunlight penetrating the water influences its pH and correspondingly bass positions somewhat," points out Fears. "The sun's reaction with plankton and things in the water is what affects the pH, and consequently, the brighter the sky, the higher the pH will rise. That will affect the bass too."

"Usually, in the winter, the pH is fairly stable, because there is very little runoff of acidic rain water," notes the former biologist. Later on during the spring, the normal runoff will affect the pH more than at any other time of the year. It can become stratified in a lake or river more easily, and the bass positions may be more affected then."

"Temperature and current have a lot to do with where the bass are located after a front," says Fears, "but the bass definitely react to pH more than they do to any other factor!"

"The pH level physically affects bass more," he explains. "It determines how aggressive they are and how much and how often they need to feed. It dictates where they are going to feed."

Although lakes are usually clearest in the winter, vegetation is minimal and seldom grows much in cold water. Because the plankton is not reproducing, the pH levels are usually lower. Add to that the deeper light penetration in clear water, and bass tend to move deeper.

A cold front early in the year will usually slow the fish down, and they'll be harder to catch. They may move to the deeper breaks in 15 to 18 feet of water at that time of year. Depending on the lake, they may even be deeper. If you know where an area held bass prior to a front coming through, then you should go back into that area. You usually have to keep working that same location, and work it much harder and longer to establish a pattern.

A jig-and-pig often works for such conditions, and so do crankbaits with shad-type patterns. Lure with a chartreuse color or those with a lot of white or gray in them to generate flash are productive at times. Most successful anglers will rely on the same size lure on both sides of the front. Many will opt for large lures which seem to attract bigger fish. Fronts don't seem to affect the size of productive baits.

If the front stays on and blows through, a high pressure dome settles over the area. After four or five days, fish down deep might become catchable because they are more adjusted to that depth. The time it takes for them to fully adjust varies with water temperature, activity levels of the fish and the particulars of that front. Normally, it takes three days or so for the fishing to come back.

Once the fish come back up, they'll readjust, but they'll be a little deeper than normal. If you were catching them in five feet of water

Cloudy skies during winter weather generally result in good fish catching opportunities. Prior to the front, bass will feed aggressively and anglers may do well then.

before the front, you might catch them in seven because that is where they're more comfortable now. They progressively proceed down to the deeper water with each front.

After the winter has set in, fish set up for the cold fronts. They stay on the steep shorelines where all they have to do when the front hits is move vertically. This location will serve all their needs, including food. They'll move in on a point with tall trees when the front is gone and will come up to feed on shad in the tops of those trees. They will migrate vertically because they don't want to go a long way then.

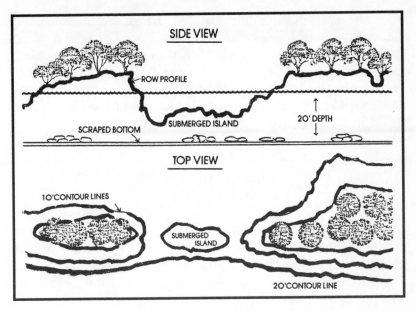

FIGURE 8 - Deep water bass tend to hold on submerged islands (humps) rather than on steep sloping banks. In a pit situation like this, expect to find concentrations of largemouth on the submerged island.

Bass tend to conserve energy and just wait for the front to pass. A big group of fish is often in a negative feeding mood, but sometimes you can get some bonanza fish during cold fronts by exploring the small pockets.

Geographical Effects

If cover is minimal and the water is extremely clear, bass will usually move deeper and search out rock structure. On northern lakes, bass become more accustomed to cold fronts, so the change affects them to a lesser degree than it does the fish further south. Fears has noticed a slight difference in the frontal effects on bass geographically.

"Florida fish, especially, are notorious for having a very fragile disposition; fronts affect them very adversely," he says. "They say down there that if someone sneezes north of the state line, the bass will turn off for three days."

"The water temperature may not change, but it is just very difficult to catch Florida bass after a front," says Fears. "Those fish are affected more than others I've fished around the country. A lake in Florida might also drop 8 to 10 degrees after a cold front. It won't stay that low for long, but it will really turn those fish off."

That doesn't seem to apply to the species of Florida bass, just those in the state, according to Fears. He frequently fishes Sam Rayburn Reservoir which has the Florida bass species, yet those fish can be caught after a front just by changing fishing tactics a little.

Bass Frontal Physics

When bass retreat to the depths quickly, their whole bladder balance is changed, according to some biologists. When a fish moves 30 feet down, its bladder air compresses and goes to exactly half its size. The fish's flotation, or its buoyancy, is relative to the volume in that bladder. When it's squeezed to half its size, it takes quite some time for the bass to adjust, and the colder the water, the longer it will take to adjust.

"The fish are usually working less and is belly to the bottom after a cold front, because they don't have any buoyancy," a biologist explained. "Their buoyancy is cut to about one eighth of what it once was. If they quickly go down 30 feet, they no longer float. Bass can't sit in a treetop over 30 feet of water and feed if they've been up in five feet of water, because if they do, they just sink."

Such bass usually find the spot which is most comfortable, and if it is 25 feet, they'll sink and sit on little shelves and breaks at that depth. They'll opt for the nearest flat spot they can find on the bottom. In fact, a big shallow feeding shelf in 25 feet of water may be just littered with a big school. Since they don't have the proper buoyancy, they have to work harder to swim and that really shuts them down.

CHAPTER 4

BURIED BASS DISCOVERIES

Methods For Fishing Dense Cover

A STROKE OF the paddle dislodged several hyacinth plants from the massive jam that extended three hundred yards back. We "notched" the edge of the canopy in three other places before we quietly anchored ten feet away from our creation to await bass movement.

King-size shiners were rigged on 5/0 hooks beneath a float and tossed the short distance to the now-irregular perimeter of the hyacinth bed. My partner and I carefully guided each of two lively baitfish into the notches and fed out line as the bobbers disappeared beneath the plants at the back of the pockets. The shiners swam another 10 to 15 feet back under the canopy before pausing.

Our reels were set on free spool and we settled back to "line watch". The purpose of the floats were to keep the bait fish off the abundant bottom entanglements in the flooded reservoir. We couldn't see them and the bass hopefully wouldn't notice the presence of a bobber snuggled up into the dangling hyacinth roots.

We watched...and waited. The late afternoon sun had only settled five degrees or so toward the horizon when tugs on two of the lines caught our attention. Instantaneously a portion of the floating plant bed rustled some 20 feet back from the cover's edge.

We were both on our feet poised for a hook set as line continued to slowly vanish from our level wind reels. It was difficult to determine which line led to the fish that had made such an impressive bulge in the canopy. We each stopped the progression of the largemouths toward the far reaches of the cover with our hook sets. The two fish were quickly worked out of the thicket without hanging up.

The pair of four pounders were being admired between the landing and live well when I noticed line peeling off another reel. I quickly dropped the fish into the box and grabbed for the active rod and reel. This fish swam out of the cover toward me, and I reeled in the slack line. The 25-pound test monofilament popped on my hook set into the heavy fish beneath the boat.

I had just began to rerig when my partner stood up and came back hard with his rod tip. Quickly he added that bass to the live well and before he could get another bait back on the rod, his other outfit had a strike. The action continued for five more minutes as we caught another five bass. Then they quit.

We waited probably 45 minutes as our eight-inch shiners prowled the dark depths back under the canopy. My partner only muttered a couple of words while he intensely studied each line twitch. Finally, a school of largemouth again moved in to the area and made quick work of our baitfish fare. We landed 15 bass in all during the two skirmishes and released them as the diminishing light ended our day. Our time spent that afternoon on Lake Oklawaha in central Florida was less than one and a half hours.

The largemouth apparently were buried far back under the surface cover and moved to the edge periodically to feed. They would then move back under the canopy to a "safe area", one providing some degree of protection. Undoubtedly the low light levels and serenity found within a dense vegetative habitat are a "safe area" to rest after feeding.

The jungle-like terrain in highly vegetated areas tend to keep a school together longer than would minimal cover. Weed-bound largemouth tend to school by year-class (age), and the weight of the fish that day varied by about three pounds. According to fisheries biologists, by the time bass reach four years of age that's not unusual.

From a special vantage point, I've often noticed large schools of bass buried in heavy vegetation along stream and lake shores. My scuba diving experiences on shallow, weed-laden waters has enabled me to take a close look at the aquatic environment, and it usually has abundant masses of water hyacinths and a maze of trails through hydrilla and coontail.

A couple of things are more apparent regarding weed-bound

Anglers that fish along weedlines and cast parallel to them are usually productive. Bulrushes and cattails provide dense habitat for bass.

bass when viewed in their own environment. What may appear impenetrable from above the water line could offer fairly wide open expanses beneath. Naturally, the actual density of submerged vegetation is totally independent of floating plant-life like hyacinths, water cabbage, or duckweed.

Floating Canopy Techniques

Floaters found through many waterways in the United States usually drift to the windward or current-swept side until contained.

Hydrilla, coontail or other submergent vegetation attracts the entire food chain, right up to the predator bass. While small bass can be found throughout the patches of aquatic weeds, lunkers require more protection in terms of depth and cover.

Often some emergent vegetation or other cover will trap the "free-spirited" floaters and, in seemingly no time, build a massive canopy. Largemouths moving into such environments have no limitations on their movements.

Water hyacinths are probably the most commonly distributed floating plant species in the southern part of the country. Their broad, shiny dark green leaves and bluish-white flowers can form a canopy that completely shades what lies below. The bottom however, is extremely important to the productivity of such cover.

In some areas, a single plant will produce several thousand new plants in a year. That much vegetation will quickly cover creek channels and structure-laden coves and canals.

The best spot among dense hyacinths that look alike is one that abuts emergent cover, such as trees, posts, reeds, etc. "Structure on structure" attracts largemouth and can be easily found. Submarining shiners, as discussed earlier, is an effective way to deal with the bass that move about under the hyacinths.

Duckweed is common throughout the U.S. and is the smallest and simplest of all flowering plants. It is frequently found on waters that are high in nutrients. Duckweed does pose unique problems to anglers trying to penetrate the light green "skin" that a windward shoreline or cove would sport.

A lure or bait must drop through the mat of plants to reach the bass that move about below. For that reason, a heavy jig or lead-headed worm that can drop through the "sticky" surface cover may be productive. A heavy weedless spoon can also be effective when fished slowly through the canopy. Bass will explode on the near-surface affair, blowing the minute plants everywhere.

The most fun way to entice several largemouth from duckweed,though, is by tossing a heavy rubber topwater plug on top of the "blanket". The pointed-nose Top Dog comes through the plant canopy easily and has a weighted tail that settles below the surface cover in between twitches. The fireworks beneath and on the weedless plug will not be forgotten.

Submergent Plant Tactics

Vegetation that builds up totally beneath the surface is different. Waterways often become clogged with the influx of a fast growing plant species, such as the common hydrilla, milfoil and coontail. However, "alleys" do exist throughout most beds of submerged plants. Pockets, holes and trails may not be observable from the angler's viewpoint, but they are there.

Bass use such "roadways" in their feeding movements, and locating the right ones can enhance an angler's thrills. Orange Springs, Florida guide Dan Thurmond once told me of his favorite way to find those best trails in heavy cover.

A lake that has a fluctuating water level and abundant submerged vegetation can be a problem to most fishermen. Management policies on such bodies of water are usually an attempt to keep access open to navigation in shallows that are prone to being totally clogged. Where boat traffic is insufficient to keep open trails through the stuff, chemicals are used.

Thurmond has found those access trails through matted hydrilla to be productive only after the water level has risen and covers all the vegetation. When two feet of water cover the majority of the plant bed and a four-foot deep by six-foot wide trail goes through it, you can imagine where the bass will be moving.

The lunker bass guide will note the presence of such potential hotspots before the water level rises. He'll then toss shiners rigged with bobbers or light-weight swimming worms along the trails for maximum action. Spoons fished over the abundant submerged vegetation are also effective in the boat lanes.

Although the range of hydrilla extends across 2/3 of the country, coontail is even more commonly distributed. Unlike most submerged aquatic plants, coontail has no roots and is easily pulled loose from the sediment. It is attached to the bottom with modified stems and has fine branches that provide habitat for aquatic insects and shelter for small fish.

Crankbaits and vibrating plugs fished over a bed of coontail are often productive. Texas Shad, Rattle Trap, and Hot Spot slab-type baits are quickly retrieved over the vegetation to remain weed-free and draw an impulse strike. Buoyant diving crankbaits are fished with a jerk-stop-jerk retrieve.

They are pulled down until they hit the vegetation and then allowed to float back toward the surface. Then after the slight pause, they are again pulled forward until hitting the coontail. Bass will usually strike the plug as it slowly ascends and forward motion is stopped.

Emergent Vegetation Techniques

Emergent cover is different from both the floating and submergent varieties in what it offers below the surface. The habitat below would probably surprise someone that has not donned a mask and snorkel or scuba gear to check it out.

Cattails, bulrushes, maidencane, reeds, etc. can all seem impenetrable on the surface. Look below and you'll realize that even a huge bass can easily navigate through the stems of most emergent plants. The stalks of such a weed jungle seem to fan out at the surface. That only makes such terrain more difficult to fish.

Better than the totally submerged, thick plant masses, bass love structures with lots of cover above and mobility below. In fact, they'll

Bigger bass will either be buried within, or when accessible to the angler, generally be deeper than the yearlings. Lily pads are excellent habitat for trophy bass.

spend a majority of their time in the "less-confused" aquatic scene provided by emergent cover. They can feed easier where the forage cannot plunge into the mass of weeds to easily escape.

Vast fields of fragrant water-lily are spread throughout shallow waters in the eastern United States. Like other pads, such as Spatter-dock, floating-leaf species provide excellent cover for invertebrates and fish. Fishing bonnets can be frustrating though.

Certain techniques and lures can minimize hangups and result in additional catches. Working the fringes of the pad bed is a wise approach initially. Bass will often position themselves just inside of the bed within striking distance of a baitfish school cruising the perimeter in open water.

Schools of threadfin shad, for example, have an aversion to penetrating highly vegetated areas. They'll move about in sun-brightened open water and do a right turn when encountering shady grounds. They'll not venture into dense weed beds or under a surface canopy. The fact that they sport reflective silver scales is reason to believe that shad are less vulnerable in open water and when the sun is shining over the area.

Weedless lures, a must for pad beds, should be cast deeper into the pockets and holes, once the perimeter has been thoroughly checked. Rubber plugs seem to bounce over the floating leaves resulting in less entanglements, and one with a pointed nose is ideal for coming through the bonnet jungles without hassle. Be prepared, though, when the lure that has crawled across the surface pads touches down on water!

Not all tall, emergent plants are similar in bass-holding characteristics. Fishery biologists, for example, have found soft-stem bulrushes to be better bass habitat than cattails. The bulrush grows in slightly deeper water and has less growth near its attachment to the bottom. A predator largemouth can easily "tuck" itself inside the lower bulrush stalks.

Flippin' techniques are extremely effective when the bass are using such cover. Long rods, up to 7 1/2 feet, and lines testing 25 pounds or more are frequently spooled onto heavy duty reels. The jig with flippin' hook is a favorite southern bait to place in front of the largemouth's nose. With rubber crawdad, flippin' worm or pork eel adornment, the productive lure is simply dropped vertically into the bulrush bed.

The bass buried in such dense, shallow cover will seldom spook with the angler's approach. Electric trolling motors can usually be used to position the boat right beside the rushes without scaring the fish. Once the jig has fallen on a limp line into the cover, a couple of twitches should inspire a nearby bass to gulp down the morsel. If not, hit the next "hole" a few feet away.

The key to effectively fishing these areas is to be ready for the explosive strikes. An angler doesn't have much time to "play" a fish in this terrain. Stout tackle is a must and patience is a virtue here. Being prepared to haul a 10-pounder over the gunwale one second after the strike may just separate the true "jungle fishermen" from the rest of the crowd.

Those fish that do bury themselves in an aquatic weed mass can be caught. Their sense of complete safety when snuggled between some reed stalks, or one hundred yards back from the edge of a floating plant canopy, makes them vulnerable. As such, weed-bound bass will often succumb to some of the specialized tactics described here.

The approach to finding and catching buried bass should be tailored to the dense vegetation being fished. Understand the options and apply various techniques, and don't give up on them.

CHAPTER 5

WEEDLINE PATROLS

Effective Presentations Where Most Fish Live

THE WEEDLINE PARTED as a huge wake formed behind a scurrying bluegill that tried to become airborne. Fifteen feet later, the surface erupted, and just as quickly as the action had started, it ended. We cast furiously all around the action to no avail.

The giant predator had apparently hit its target and retreated to the weedbed. After about 20 minutes of working the small area of weed points and pockets in the vicinity, we gave up...but not for long.

We moved away to work another area and returned to that spot about 30 minutes later. My partner and I couldn't get the huge boil out of our mind. We wanted to catch the source of it.

Again, we cast a variety of lures to the weedline, but that fish was not interested yet. After another 20 minutes of futile casting, we vacated the weedline for an hour. We were about to quit for the day, but we each wanted one last shot at that fish. We motored back over to the spot, shut off the outboard and used the electric motor to move in the last 20 yards.

My partner's first cast with a Texas-rigged worm to the weed pocket hangout of that fish was accurate. As he lifted the rod, he felt the tug and set back on it. The bass immediately shot skyward and the battle had begun. Five minutes later, I slipped the net under the nine pounder to end the tussle. The largemouth, apparently the same one that had given herself away earlier, was fat with forage that summer day.

Our perseverance paid off on that weedline inhabitant, but many bass that frequent the weed edges are not as stubborn about striking. Bass love aquatic vegetation during the summer months, because food, protection and cover are readily available. Ideal water characteristics such as pH, dissolved oxygen and temperature are conducive to active largemouth - those that are in a feeding (striking) mood.

Flippin' is one of the most productive methods for tall, dense stands of emergent vegetation, such as bulrushes, cattails, reeds, etc. In the south, they often grow to eight feet above the surface are the summer home of many concentrations of largemouth.

A large worm with "gator-type" tail rigged self-weedless is popular to drop in the thick of things. One very important trick to use on the flippin' worm rig concerns the slip sinker. In dense cover, it cannot be left to free-slide. It must be 'pegged' by inserting a round toothpick into the sinker and breaking off the tip to wedge the line, welding the worm and weight together. This will prevent their parting company when the rig is worked in the stands of dense cover.

A second trick to utilize is to lubricate the worm thoroughly with a fish attractor solution, such as Berkley Strike. That will facilitate ease of sliding it in and out of the weed stands. A dry, flexible plastic worm tends to cling to each and every stalk of reed, as the bait is removed from a hole. Lubrication of the worm, and even the jig and eel, is vital to the success of the technique.

Dense stands offer bass heavy cover in which to bury themselves. The trolling motor can be run seemingly within inches of the bass without spooking the fish. Reeds and other tall vegetation can be more closely watched for bass movement when the boat is up close. The small pockets in the weedline are where the majority of strikes will occur. The difficult to hit spots are the fishiest. Most strikes will occur on the fall. Watch the line as the bait drops through the hole.

Use a good quality, low stretch monofilament line in 20 to 30 pound test if after a trophy bass. The flippin' tackle should be heavy to withstand the rugged fishing and catching conditions. A stiff rod to set the hook and jerk the bass from its environment is vital. The reel preferred by most weed bound anglers is a baitcasting model, but some expert flippers opt for spinning reels. Use as light a sinker as possible in such cover, unless the water below is extremely deep. Hook size for the productive eight-inch worm should be 5/0.

FIGURE 9 - Use a lubricated worm or jig skirt and trailer to not only attract more bass but to allow the lure to more easily slide in and out of dense cover.

This method, although taking some skill and knowledge, is an exciting one for locating and catching bass concentrations along dense weedlines. In fact, it may be the most effective way to catch summer bass from such cover.

Inside Strategies

Many southern waters have three distinct weedlines; one where the shoreline weeds end and another on either side of a bar that skirts the perimeter. Thus, a weedbed lies in front of the shore-based weeds, leaving a small channel between the two. This is usually a deeper trough with sparse weeds bordering it. Bass use these 'road beds' to move along in search of forage.

The predator largemouth loves weedlines from which to ambush its prey. Most shallow lakes and ponds have weedlines that are extremely productive year around.

Similar areas are the boat lanes through weedbeds. Boat traffic, depth and bottom composition can have the effect of a trail through weeds and a couple of weedlines. The edges of such allies are productive spots to cast. Pockets lie off to either side, and the successful angler will work these areas slowly and very thoroughly. He'll hit all irregular features along the weed beds.

As lake waters rise, similar areas are produced which may cover shoreline vegetation. Only the taller weed masses are left just off shore. Such areas are particularly productive on windy days when waves will pound the front face of the weedline. While many bass will lie on the shore-side weedline, the more active largemouth will be found on the windward weedline, facing the blow.

Some of the masses of aquatic plant life may appear impenetrable to an angler's lures, and many fishermen will simply fish elsewhere. They are afraid of getting hung up and losing or fouling their lures. They are also concerned about losing any bass that may strike the offering. Several strikes may, in fact, be misses, but such areas harbor exceptional concentrations of largemouth.

Dollar weed, spatterdock, pickerel weed, hydrilla, elodea, coontail moss and fragrant water lilies (among others) may grow into masses of vegetation and form a distinct weedline with numerous pockets and points. The light below the dense masses is subdued, but a lure's movement above is often noticed. If the bait is kept moving when in the weeds and allowed to stay near the weedline when it moves out of them, it will attract attention.

Experience can teach you to perfect a retrieve around such cover and take advantage of the often-unnoticed concentration of bass below. Position the boat close to the weed mass that you intend to fish, and make your cast fairly short to maintain accuracy and control of the lure as it's being retrieved. The denser cover allows you to move in tighter to the quarry, and the odds of landing the bass improve as the length of line out decreases.

If the water is shallow enough behind the weedbed, a wade fisherman can effectively work that portion of the weedline. Successful waders also look for stained water clarity, hard bottoms and other structural changes that denote bass. They'll cast to the shallow side of any weed mass. They'll work the trough and pockets just off it by moving to the most optimal casting spot.

Lure selection and presentation are key to catching several bass from the "back alley." Lure balance is also extremely critical. Spinnerbaits are very popular in the trough and an unbalanced lure will become fouled easily in the grass cover. The bait should bump the weeds on the retrieve to best trigger a strike from nearby bass. The balanced spinnerbait will keep the hook in an upright position on the retrieve.

The small, shallow alley is ideal for working slower, more distinct lures. Floating worm and swimming worm rigs are both productive behind the weed beds on the near-shore weedline. Their buoyancy is effective at keeping them out of tangles and in the strike zone longer.

Weedless jig-and-eels can be effective in this habitat, and of course the weedless spoon has a well deserved reputation for attracting weed bound largemouth. Bill Norman's Weed Walker is a great bait to toss around dense weedbeds. Cast the weedless lure beyond the target opening to avoid spooking any nearby inhabitant. Inch the lure to the edge of the weedline, and let it free fall to the bottom.

Moving Strategies

Weedbeds generally begin at the shore and extend out into the water for several feet. They often grow to a drop off and stop. Other limiting factors to their spread in a lake or river is depth, water

A variety of vegetation can form dense weedlines that harbor concentrations of summer largemouth. Worms fished through the stalks are successful baits.

clarity, fertility and type of soil. When the weedline stops in deep water, it virtually eliminates the non-boater from catching fish positioned on that weedline. The deep water weed beds provide largemouth with security and plenty of forage, so it is an enticing environment to the largemouth.

When casting toward the weedline, hangups may result, particularly in those weeds that are thicker than most. Casting parallel to

Crankbaits are often effective lures to toss at weedlines. Most are surprisingly weedless.

the weedline while moving along it with the electric trolling motor is often the best way to fool several bass. To catch them when they are concentrated on the points or pockets of a weedline, the parallel caster must use stealth as he approaches the fish. Fortunately, the weedline cover often hides his presence.

The successful angler using this method moves quietly along the weedline, casting in front of the boat and bringing a lure, like my favorite Rat-L Trap, past all pockets and points of the vegetation. Isolated clumps of cover are focused on by the observant anglers. Irregular spots along a weedline are great places to hook up with a largemouth. Pockets and points both entice this predator to lie in wait for it's food. Bass, particularly big ones, will actually stake out such preferred territories.

Trolling crankbaits over and around vegetation is just one effective way to catch bass on a warm summer day. I utilized such a technique several times over the years on Fayette County Lake, and it regularly caught largemouth and lots of them.

Hydrilla-covered points and humps provide productive haunts for bass, but they can be frustrating. Hang-ups, at least temporary ones, are a way of life. In trolling such areas, they can be counted on to interrupt the operation, but you can learn to overlook such.

I made six passes by the first point to the right of the ramp at Fayette one day and had several interruptions to my troll. Eighteen were largemouth bass which were quickly landed and released. Five would have easily bested the 16-inch minimum in force at the time.

With each trolling pass that day, I became more familiar with the "lay of the land" beneath the boat. Hangups became less frequent and the bass picking better. My eyes were trained on the chart recorder with each pass, and I was learning to fish the hydrilla points and humps off that shoreline.

My shad-colored crankbaits ran at about 8 feet and that's where the bass were located that day. I've used trolling as an effective means to fish vegetation in many lakes. It may not be as exciting as other methods, but it can be more productive at times, depending on the type of cover and the location of the largemouth.

Areas where the weeds are different in some way are particularly active bass haunts that are accessible to the moving angler. An expanse of maiden cane with an isolated patch or two of pickerel weed would be an example. The bass concentrations would most probably be at the edge of the pickerel patch. The successful caster will check out the depressions, slots, points, boat lanes, clearings, etc. in and around the weed cover.

Various forms of vegetation may grow until the mass is so dense that it is virtually impenetrable for predator and angler, alike. In such clogs, bass often stick close to the outside edge or weedline. Largemouth are able to ambush their prey by holding tight to the thick weed mass, and the trolling angler may be extremely productive there.

In such locations, bass are also prone to strike at a trolled lure. The angler can cover territory quickly with the aid of an outboard or powerful electric motor, and the lure or bait can be presented to numerous bass along a weedline. The key to successful trolling is the movement of the boat adjacent to a weedline and the resultant position of the lure at all times, in bass striking territory.

Weedline bass will often hold at the edge above a sharp "break" or elevation change. In fact, this drop may be among the most distinguishable in a shallow, natural lake. As a result, the trolling angler should keep a close eye on his depth finder and have a good idea where his lure or bait is running. He can cover this breakline thoroughly and catch the more active bass that usually face the deep water.

Areas off islands or submerged bars are particularly productive trolling spots. The depth along such weedlines may be 20 feet or more, and the bottom structure is often unique. Projections from a uniform weedline and depth can hold a concentration of large-mouth. Isn't that just what most of us are looking for?

CHAPTER 6

VEGETATION TACTICAL MOVES

Fitting Lures Into The Bass Environment

VEGETATION ON A lot of lakes can be intimidating, and anglers often shy away from dense, heavy cover such as bulrushes, long-stalked grass, pads or cattails, but that is where largemouth bass are found. Ideal pH, water temperature, oxygen levels, forage and protection exists in such places and several productive techniques for largemouth living in the trenches of vegetation. Presentations and lures not up to the challenge will often force an angler to make excuses for a less than successful day. Knowing the best lures to use and successful ways to fish them is vital to establishing the best pattern on waters with abundant vegetation.

Fishing dense cover in shallow water can be most effective with surface lures or top water baits. In waters of less than five foot depths, surface baits will often entice a lunker bass to come up like thunder to the surface, an exciting moment. Such bass may be on the feed, or it may be necessary to excite them into striking. Bass in the shade and concealment of submerged or emergent vegetation will usually note the action above them, so little movement is required to disturb the surface and produce audible noise.

Many of favorite heavy cover baits do not float. While employed on the surface, they will descend to the bottom if the line becomes slack. Since the action and control of these lures is through the rod tip, a taut line is a must. A surface-worked lure in heavy cover will bring the bass to the top, making it easier for the angler to keep the bass head up and out of the entanglements below. Keeping a big bass on the surface in this case is the key to landing them.

A surface-worked lure will bring the bass to the top, making it easier to keep the bass out of entanglements.

Largemouth seem to know when they have the protection needed to escape potential predators, like us anglers. They feed in areas that provide maximum cover and entanglements, and the surface bait is an ideal lure to get at them. Surface spoons, like Norman's Weed Walker and others without the paddle wheel blade have been favorites of mine for years. A skitter, spoon-type plug rides the waters' surface best in a twitching pattern. It can ride up and over vegetation as few other lures can.

Fishing them is easy. In waters with heavy weed growth, a slow-moving bait is natural on the surface. A wake can often be seen forming behind the lure's wake. Simply keep it coming fast enough to keep the paddle wheel turning and be ready to set the hook. Guiding the lure through a bed of lily pads or other emergent vegetation takes practice and watching the line, as well as the lure, is important to prevent snags and have proper control of the bait.

Short casts in the vegetated areas are most practical, and boat movement should be minimal to prevent hangups. Casts should be made ahead of the boat as the angler works the fringes of the bonnets so that the line of retrieve will not loop behind the boat. A taut line means better lure control and a better hook set.

Big bass are particularly hard to land from dense vegetation, but having a lure that will work well and provoke the strike is a major consideration. In a thick pad bed with just a few small openings of water, for example, bass will have little time to focus on the lure and will strike instinctively, at times even missing the lure. When they do take it solidly, some may be lost trying to get them out of the entanglements.

Weeds that grow to the surface of a lake and then mat up and clog the water are particularly hard to fish. To be an effective producer in this type of cover, the lure must ride the surface easily over any heavy growth of aquatic plants.

In the densest vegetation, the retrieve is started just before the lure lands on the water. Baits that ride on their backs with the hook riding up, away from the vegetation are ideal selections. Bass may follow this type of lure for 20 feet in heavy weeds before pouncing on it. Once the big bass has struck and is coming toward the boat, try to prevent her from diving into the heavy stuff. As the size of catch approaches giant proportions, however, that's not always possible.

A trailer hook added to these offerings may increase their effectiveness. Hangups may increase in its wobbling across the surface, but so may the catch rate of bass.

My favorite "contact" lures for bass in vegetation are surface-buzzing spinner baits. They generally have a blade design that pops it up on the surface and allows the fisherman to crank it back at a very slow pace, keeping it on top at all times. A buzzer that moves slow and sprays water above the surface even at the slowest speeds is deadly. Used around dense grass patches, they are normally fished with the rod tip held high. Again, the angler should begin reeling just before the lure hits the water.

Buzz baits are effective in both pockets and on point of vegetation. The retrieve should usually be slow, but can be speeded up to trigger bass into striking. The two elements that make the baits successful are its noise and any contact made. The lures must be emitting sound and be making contact with the cover where bass may be living.

In emergent vegetation, it important for the lure to be in contact with the structure. "Bumping" such cover will result in some exciting explosions. Strikes occur just after the lure bumps a piece of vegetation near the bass.

Different buzz baits move in a retrieval trajectory that varies. Some with two blades move right to left as they approach the angler while others, like Norman's Triple Buzz moves from left to right while being retrieved. The turning of the blade provides a 'torque' of sorts that causes the lure to move off a straight course.

If an angler wishes to fish a particular side of the cover, the task is simplified. He can select a buzz bait that runs right and fish it to the left side of the cover as his boat moves forward. That lure should always return to make contact with the cover. An angler in the back of the boat may want to throw a buzz bait which exhibits a reverse torque so that he can more effectively work the other side of the cover.

Sound is especially important in stained or roily waters, since visibility could be minimal. The main attractor under these conditions requires the right sound. In tuning the lures, often the more used or worn the lure the better sound quality that is produced. Use an old one around the vegetation.

Another productive pattern in overwhelming habitat during the summer is flippin' small, isolated rush clumps. In stained waters, fishing depths of only four or five feet can be successful. On the hottest days, the best pattern for vegetation-bound bass may be

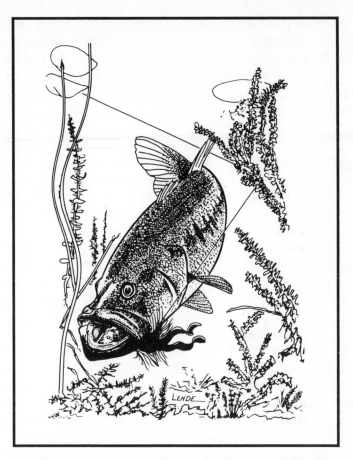

FIGURE 10 - Bass inhabit a variety of vegetation, yet an angler fishing the right lures can catch them. Flippin' a jig adorned with Strike Rind is one of the best ways to catch bass from dense weedbeds.

fishing the densest buggy-whip patches or grass beds. Even in dense cover, hot-weather fish will be deeper, in five or six feet of water.

If unfamiliar with the water, I'll move in close to such vegetation and check the water depth and type-bottom present, prior to fishing the area. Bass prefer a clean bottom, and even if the area is so dense with vegetation that it has decomposed plants on the bottom, a sandy soil may lie beneath. Sandy bottoms encourage the growth of rushes or "buggy whips", as some call them.

The best patches of rushes, reeds or any other emergent structure can be found by eye-balling the height. The good fishing areas generally have the tallest vegetation growth due to the optimal soil conditions. Sandy bottom, for example, is extremely fertile, causing the reed jungle to grow to taller elevations. The healthiest waters have the healthiest forage base and, correspondingly, the biggest bass.

The presentation must be smooth and quiet, and timing is everything. Begin the flip by pulling off enough line with your left hand until the bait is at the water's surface. Now, raise the rod tip so that the bait lifts up off the water's surface and starts to swing toward you. With an underhand swing, arch the lure in a pendulum motion toward the target.

You can control the excess line with your left hand which should move back toward the reel, as the lure is flipped toward the cover. When flippin' in heavy cover, turn the line loose at the right moment and try to let the bait fall to the bottom directly below its ideally soft landing. You might have to slowly "yo-yo" the bait three or four times to entice a bass.

If you cannot attract a strike on your offering, realize that many non-predator species or rough fish won't bite bass lures. Rough fish may travel en masse and knock several stalks at once when they move. Instead of simply shaking one reed or a small clump, one will often spook and start a chain reaction. Such bumping extravaganzas aren't indicative of bass. Largemouth are typically more curious, and they'll remain in the vegetation.

Whether you approach the weeds by trolling, flipping or casting buzzers or spoons, you'll likely find some receptive bass.

CHAPTER 7

BRUSHY ESCAPES

Analyzing Wood Habitats

THE SURFACE TALKS. The environmental expression above the water often reveals the secrets that lie beneath the surface. On lakes with lots of wood, that's important. The best pattern may be obvious to a few, but a flooded forest can certainly puzzle the majority of fishermen. Anglers seldom realize they need help in reading surface characteristics and learning a water's personality.

A forest of submerged trees often defines a route for food fish and their predators. An ideal location is a 'cut' from a large open water portion of a lake to a smaller, but also open water area. I found one such prime spot a few years back. Flooded trees with floating hyacinths trapped between them established the boundaries.

I had taken four bass from the cut earlier in the day but had found no consistent action. The few fish present were feeding in the deep, in 20 feet of water. A shade line below the floating plants existed in conjunction with the treeline and further prevented encroachment by the forage schools that periodically moved through the cut.

Fishing was relatively slow and the late afternoon sun was heading for the horizon when I suggested to my partner that we move back to the cut. We motored over to it and, as we approached, could hear the commotion caused by several large fish feeding on the surface. The bass were popping schools of small shad that had been chased and funneled into the cut from the large open water area.

Schools of bass larger than I've ever seen were feeding on top and they seemed to be all over the cut. The action continued for 45 minutes, and I later discovered it had paralleled a major solunar

Partially submerged shoreline cover harbors numerous largemouth. The key to catching fish from them is the lure and its presentation.

period starting at 6 p.m. that day. Plenty of schools of five and six pound fish moved into and through the 100-foot wide cut, but the eight to ten-pound bass schooling on top that afternoon were awe inspiring to this angler.

At any one time during that period, there were three to four separate and distinct schools slashing shad on top, and each school had four to eight fish on the surface at all times while they moved through the cut. It was obvious that the treeline and hyacinth line were a boundary.

As the large schools of bass pushed the forage to the edges of the cut, the action would then move back toward the more open water

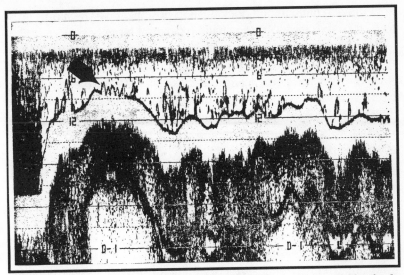

FIGURE 11 - Submerged stumps (shown on top of the hump) are great habitat for the largemouth and its forage. Locating the productive structures in the presence of a rolling hill terrain is often possible.

in the center of the cut. Many shad were knocked on top of the hyacinths, but they would not venture back under the floating plants.

Some 35 bass were hooked and released, most were over two pounds. We returned all to the water except for three that were deeply hooked. The 'waves' of schooling bass that moved through the cut that afternoon kept our rods arched and even our arm muscles straining. The action was a vivid reminder of the importance of relating surface expression to the quarry we were seeking.

Sometimes a very subtle difference in the brush environment can make a tremendous difference in the catch. I once found several small bass holding on willow trees and buck brush lying off isolated islands in a reservoir. The fish were numerous, but they were small. A move from the highly-pressured islands to main shore willow points and isolated buck bushes with adjacent deep water proved a winner.

The bushy trees in two to four feet of water had short moss or algae growing on their shady side, and they also had bass, big ones in the deeper areas. Worms and jigs could be flip cast into the shady area of each ball-shaped buck bush. Those bushes which only grow to four or five feet, offered shade to several large bass.

Finding the right structure is vital. I was fishing with an old friend one day on a 2000-acre impoundment when the importance of surface expression was again emphasized. My partner and I had been working some shallow pad fields with little success when we decided to forego further early morning chasing of the lunker bass. Instead, we moved to a 'honey hole' of his that was loaded with average-sized fish.

The ten minute boat trip put us into some submerged timber, which from a casual observance resembled one thousand other areas on this lake. But it was different. A change in depth was not apparent as we slowly moved across two open areas to tie up to a large tree which emerged from the water near others.

The next two hours of fishing from that location were 'slow' according to my friend. We hooked and released 15 bass between two and three pounds each, and another 25 that averaged around 12 inches. My partner had been catching double that in his previous four trips to the lake!

The reason why the bass were in that area became obvious after studying the topography. The treeline was a migration path for feeding largemouth. The path made a turn at that particular location and held bass longer than the straight tree line. In the middle of the bend, a point of trees separated or split the migration path into two parts. The fish were on this location for several hours each day, and a mussel bed or other bottom structure was non-existent.

That productive area provided a good ambush point for bass, and the treeline apparently limited the movement of the smaller forage fish by defining a structural path to move along. The trees were, in many cases, only four feet apart. Yet, to the forage, the treeline may as well have been a brick wall. Small forage schools are usually very reluctant to penetrate such cover, and this trait makes foraging easier for the largemouth and other gamefish.

Wood Patterns

Today's successful anglers must know the various kinds of woods and the important differences between each. Knowing the usual

Flooded timber in the middle of a lake may be difficult to read for the average angler. Successful ones, however, learn to analyze the surface expression to determine what lies below.

relationship between each can 'clue in' the thinking angler to a pattern at times.

Most anglers know that submerged cedar trees generally provide better fishing than, say, flooded pine trees. The pine will rot much quicker and have fewer small branches to provide cover for forage fish. But, have you ever analyzed a forest of flooded palm trees?

Some palm trees have smooth trucks while others have tough, rugged fronds hanging on the trunks. The bark texture also varies from tree to tree, but one rule can be made. The more cover that a tree provides, the more forage and other fish will be found.

The water's surface can also be read even though nothing is emerging from it. Wave action can tip off the observant angler to bottom conditions in a flooded forest and thus help him determine exactly what is below.

A friend and I were on a small reservoir one spring when a strong southerly wind came up, turning the timber-strewn lake into large swells and white caps. But, upon close observation, we noticed that not all waves were 'breaking' in the same manner across the timber flats. Some were short and choppy while others were long, swell-type movements.

The presence of an underwater hump with small brush had been detected. Actually, it was the remnants of a dike of spoil from activity that occurred before the flooding of the forested reservoir. The wind was pushing waves right into it and they were breaking on top of the shallow, brushy hump in a relatively deep area of the lake.

We assumed that baitfish would also soon be stacked up there against the brushy hump due to the strong winds. Bass could not be far behind, we reasoned, and they were not. Within the hour we boated five largemouths, including a six-pounder from the windward side of the hump!

The vast submerged brush in the lake and its newness to us had hidden the hump's identity, but the strong winds had uncovered the secret. Surface waves can also reveal such things as submerged brush or trees that reach to just below the surface, and bottom character- istics such as mud, silt, etc. Mud and silt are easily disturbed and a check of the visibility near the surface should help to identify the bottom soil type.

While too low a visibility may sometimes result in poor fishing, at other times it actually helps. Many anglers head for submerged timber in dirty water on an ultra-clear reservoir to catch creek bass. Conversely, water with a visibility of an inch or so will drive off most anglers, since the sight feeders such as bass may be hard to catch. In that water though, according to fisheries researchers, those bass may be able to see up to six inches and feel the vibrations of a lure much further than that.

Another significant clue to the potential of the wooded environ- ment below is current. Detecting a current can be stringer-saving to a knowledgeable angler. The tilt or slant of emergent brush can reveal the general direction of the water flow. Often a glance at a specific location will reveal stickups bordering open water that are flapping in the current. Moving water to many fish means easier feeding, a cooler more hospitable environment to stay in, and sometimes deeper water and bigger bass.

The entire water could be covered with floating water plants, yet an observant angler would find the deeper submerged creek channel from the clue. The surface expression in the flooded woods often provides the keys to memorable bass patterns!

CHAPTER 8

DOCKSIDE DUTY

Selecting The Best Lures And Presentations

FOR MANY ANGLERS, fishing docks and piers can be a frustrating experience. Inaccurate casts around the man-made structure are usually not forgiving. Pilings always seem to be in the way of a cast, a retrieve, or a fish battle; and then there's the dog barking from its backyard kingdom, which includes the wooden runway and dock.

Up close presentations are effective with skippin' baits and the right equipment. Underhand casts which skip the bait to its mark are often more difficult that the sidearm tosses from afar. A bass boat with a casting platform, a spinning reel, and a relatively short spinning rod will enable the angler to either fire or skip the bait back under the structure with the underhand motion.

Obviously, the rod tip can't hit the water as it swings by, thus the need for the extra height that a casting platform provides. How accurately the bait is placed is critical to enticing the fish. Anglers who are accustomed to casts somewhere between overhand and sidearm need practice to be proficient at this.

Another method to present a bait to nearby fish, and one that the average bass fishing public is probably more familiar with, is flippin.' For those who appreciate the value of a quiet approach, docks can yield great catches of bass. Docks in moderately stained waters can be approached by careful anglers who avoid bumping into the support pilings. Otherwise, careless boat positioning will usually spook bass located beneath the structure.

Flippin' is very efficient at presenting the lure to dock-bound largemouth, since very little time is required to move the bait to another spot. The lure is seldom out of productive water, as it might be when using the conventional casting method. When a largemouth grabs the bait, the stout rod will provide the leverage needed to hoist it away from the dock pilings and the submerged cross members before an entanglement occurs.

The typical dock bass may "sock" the lure hard or stop it and just hold on. It may mouth it or run deeper into the dock support structure with the morsel. When a bass grabs the bait, simply set the hook quickly and haul it out away from the obstruction. The bass will quickly tie knots around a piling, never to be seen, if its head can't be powered upward immediately.

Outside Rumblings

Bass can be caught at the edges of the dock perimeter, but the lure must trigger an instantaneous strike. Most presentations that "call bass out" from their shelter are either slow and authentic-looking or erratic and impulse-generating. The former are usually plastic snakes, lizard or water dog imitations, jig-and-eels or other slow-motion type lures that are brought along the shady edge of the dock. Bass are going after such fare to fill their stomachs, plain and simple.

Impulse strikes are generated generally by lures such as buzzbaits, crankbaits or the like, that will move along rapidly and bump into the support pilings. They create racket and disturbance and invite a bass in the darkened canopy to slam into the "out-of-control" passerby. Contact with a succession of pilings will allow the bass to plan its ambush of the intruder.

I've found buzzbaits easy to present to a row of support posts, but you have to know which way the lure moves on the retrieve for maximum contact with the pilings. The buzzing blade, whether double or triple, moves to one side on a straight retrieve. That is due to the curvature of the blade and direction of turn, and correspondingly, the torque created by its twirling.

Some buzzers move to the right and others move to the left. One cast should tell you which way the lure runs. Obviously, another buzzbait with the blades turning in the opposite direction will move

Piers, docks and boat houses come in all shapes and sizes. Presenting the lure deep beneath the lower ones may result in a large bass.

in the opposite direction. For working both sides of a dock effectively, it is best to have a right-running buzzer for the left side and a left-running lure for the right side.

You want that lure to continually bounce off each support post as it is retrieved parallel to the side of the dock or runway. Expect a strike just after each "bump." That's when the bass is most likely to try and kill the lure. The bump and grind may be an irritant to the largemouth tucked safely in its home, or there might be other motivations involved to make the bass explode on the bait, but it will.

Crankbaits work similarly, but they are not as weedless. They can be tuned with a pair of pliers to run in one direction or the other by adjusting the tie eye on their bill or nose. The hard crank-and-bump retrieve is highly effective on the outskirts of a dock, but hang-ups occur. That's unfortunate. Once a lure has become entangled, you have to go in and get it, and that may disturb what bass are left under the dock.

"Lively" Presentations

Dockside presentations may differ after dark, depending on the most effective type of habitat present and the availability and movement of forage. For example, massive schools of red minnows gather collectively each spring on some lakes, and smart bass anglers rise early or stay out late to take advantage of the two to four-week long event.

Lights on the end of a dock can mean a good stringer. A guide told me of one where the lights were automatically turned on at 4 a.m. each day. Light penetration into crystal clear water down to six feet began attracting red minnows. Tiny 2-inch forage fish were 'drawn' out of the darkness by the thousands. A healthy influx of bugs around the lights were the siren.

Red minnows formed a swirling circle below the boat house lights, which were placed just three feet from the water's surface. Millions of baitfish churned the water as though caught up in an invisible blender. The red minnows were "running," and bass would gorge themselves on the morsels until satisfied beyond full.

Each night during that period, locals typically got up early to experience the unique action. My guide friend was no exception. He arrived at a friend's house at 5 a.m., and they walked out on the dock. Sure enough, a circling mass of minnows attracted to near-surface lights had dark shapes cruising beneath the swirls. The black forms moving through the light rays were largemouth bass ranging in size from one to three pounds.

Preparation for the impending action began not at 4 a.m., but a day earlier, when the two anglers seined 200 red minnows from the shallow reeds near shore. The bait gathering took only an hour and the men were amply stocked for the night's action.

The most effective presentation was to drop their baitfish into the midst of the swirling minnows and then lower them to a point about 2 feet beneath the mass. Each man had an immediate strike and battled a scrappy largemouth, which they quickly landed. They rebaited and again placed their minnows below the bait concentration. They hooked up with a couple of two pounders, and the action never stopped until they had amassed a quick limit in just 35 minutes, averaging about two pounds apiece.

Often, kneeling down to cast beneath a man-made structure is a means to more accuracy. Casting the wooden pilings and support structures with a lure that makes contact with them will trigger strikes from bass that seldom venture far from the shadows to chase a meal.

The somewhat unique experience of fishing the red minnow runs below lighted docks takes place in the darkness and dissolves at dawn. The first hour at dusk and the last one before dawn are the best times for this particular action. The minnow masses disperse when the sun shows up, and so do the bass.

Catching dock bass on live bait or artificials may be a new experience but it doesn't have to intimidate an angler. Some careful planning regarding lure selection and presentation, though, is usually in order.

Dock-Bound Presentation

Hot weather and bright sun seem to concentrate bass far back under some docks, making them difficult for the non-boater to catch. Presenting a lure to the shade-seekers, when not having the cast and retrieve positioning freedom of a boat, is possible. You'd better know all possible obstructions, though, to keep from losing your lures.

Floating structures may have anchors, tie-down cables, ladders, and lights, which eliminate accurate presentations from dockside. Carpet pieces, cane poles, minnow traps, dangling boat-hoist straps and other temporary or permanent features may also make the perfect cast and retrieve difficult. Willow brush or Christmas tree "plantings" beneath docks to create a holding area for fish are also possible hang-ups.

The dock-walker who moves quietly can make accurate underhand casts into the darkness beneath him. A very effective presentation for largemouth holding under floating docks is to bring a crankbait back under the foam supports. The lure is first cast past the structure's far corner from a mid-way point, and then the angler walks on to the opposite end prior to beginning the retrieve.

The rod is thrust into the water around that corner of the dock and the retrieve is begun. The lure's retrieval path then is beneath the floating supports. The crankbait can even be tuned to run further inside of the darkened environment by adjusting the tie eye on the front of the bait. Take pliers and bend the eye in the opposite direction that you want the bait to run on the retrieve.

Dock-side patterns are often the most productive, and I'll usually head toward the man-made structure to check it out. It doesn't take long...unless you get into a large concentration of bass.

CHAPTER 9

TACTICS ON THE ROCKS

Methods To Catch Largemouth

ROCKS ARE UNIQUE structures that are food-intensive and as a result, attract bass. Special methods are needed to effectively catch fish from rocky cover. Techniques, strategies, and lures to develop the most productive pattern must be carefully selected. Boat positioning and lure presentations are important in order to catch bass from various types of rock structure.

One way to approach rocky bluffs is to use three different size (lip) crankbaits: shallow, deep, and double-deep. By using all three, you are covering different depths. It's wise to alternate approximately every 20 casts. Make long parallel casts down the side of the bluff, again alternating speeds until you find what the bass want. Keep the boat right next to the bluff, if possible, so that you are fishing close to it at all times.

A second productive pattern for bluff fishing is casting a 1/2 oz. or larger single spin spinnerbait straight into the bluff and letting it "helicopter" down the side of the bluff, slowly pumping it ever so often. This can be particularly deadly in colder weather. A third method that successful anglers often employ on bluffs is to flip the bank with a jig and pig. Simply swim the pig down the side of the bluff.

On creek banks, go to the outside bends toward exposed rock or where debris may collect in rock pockets. About 80 percent of bass in rocky creeks are caught in the outside bends, and the current there is the big factor. Water usually washes out dirt and leaves an undercut on the outside bends, whether it is submerged or a bank

The author has often established productive patterns on man-dug pits that leave rock strewn about. Such rock structure is often the most productive on the lake.

you can see. A rocky area here is a natural ambush spot for bass.

I like to work a crankbait along flooded creeks that I have first located with sonar. Once you mark a creek with the recorder and buoys, you can look back and read the layout. Then you can concentrate your fishing on the rocky outside bends and where the channel runs close to points. These are the best holding points for bass.

Many times, you will find parts of a rocky creek channel silted in, and when you can find the parts that are not silted, these are prime holes for bass. Spend a little extra time just working these silted creek channels and you might have yourself a bonanza hole.

The first thing to do when fishing rip rap is to cruise down the side of the rip rap from one end to the other looking for the deepest water or channels next to rocks. The corners by bridges or any change in rock configuration always produce well. Use crankbaits or spinnerbaits and cast almost parallel to the rip rap. With a worm or jig, cast straight into the rip rap.

When fishing rocky bars, you can usually find fish on the down-current side where an eddy forms and makes a dead water pocket. Two methods that are particularly effective for fishing bars are the kneel-and-reel technique and the do nothin' system. On the first method, use a 7 foot rod and deep diving crankbait, and cast as far out over the bar as possible. Then stick the rod tip down in the water and very simply kneel down and reel.

An easier, yet very productive method is to use the 'do nothing' worm rig. Position the boat on the down side of a bar which is usually where the deepest point on the bar lies. Cast up on the bar, past where an eddy should be, and work the do nothing rig back through the eddy. If that doesn't work, fish up the bar to see if the bass are feeding on it or on humps that might be on the bar.

Another very effective method pattern for bars, especially in moving current, is vertically jigging a spoon. Get right over the top of a rocky point and jig the spoon right under the boat. Using short hops and watching your line closely for the pickups will fool many bass.

Roadbed Basics

Rocky underwater roadbeds can be very productive almost any time of year. In cold weather, the surface will warm and bass will move up on them. In early spring, roadbeds are very good migration routes for bass to use to and from deep water. They usually have ditches, stumps, and bridges which are all good holding places.

Turn on your sonar equipment and go to work with marker buoys. Once you use the crossing pattern with your chart recorder and mark the road, you will have a good picture of how the road lays. It will show you dropoffs and old bridges, etc. When fishing old road beds, many times you can find sections of ditches that have not silted in, and these make excellent little dropoffs that hold fish. Always fish across the roadbeds.

Rock slides along bluff areas are always good jig and frog areas. In water colder than 60 degrees, the combination is hard to beat around any type of rock cover. The key is to flip or pitch the bait to help keep it from always getting hung up in the rocks. Tiny plastic worms and tube-type fare can also be excellent baits for chunk rock banks. Such places are great pre-spawn areas, and bass may be in the shallows chasing crawdads. They can be caught on crawfish-colored cranks then.

During warm weather, rip-rap is a prime spot for concentrations of bass. Rip-rap can be good year round, but it's a great place during the summer months. Use topwater baits, and work them right along the bank. Rock wing dams on large rivers, like the Arkansas River in the Little Rock/Pine Bluff area, are great places when the current is right. Crankbaits and worms usually complete the pattern then.

Rock-strewn impoundments with numerous bluffs exist throughout the hilly areas of the country and in the western states. Most successful anglers fish parallel to the bluffs with a crankbait. They'll attempt to keep the bait digging into the rocks on the retrieve. The key to catching bass is to maintain bottom contact. Fish smaller rock outcropping when stained water exists or when there is a lot of wind and wave action present. Otherwise, the gravel-size rock may not hold many fish.

When fishing rocks in high winds, always retrieve baits opposite the wind direction. Don't cast them into the wind. When flipping, however, fish into the wind, and you'll have better boat control.

I look for a few other specific things when fishing a rocky impoundment, whether it's in Minnesota or Florida (yes, there are some in the deep south). Many waters with high concentrations of rocks are relatively clear. The best water color is accordingly often found toward the headwaters (furthest from the dam).

Rocks in dingier waters are usually more productive. Crayfish and other forage feel more comfortable and safe in an environment such as that. Too, water color (and visibility) is indicative of the fertility present in the body of water. The presence of algae usually means abundant forage fish that love to dine on the stuff.

The food base in rocky reservoirs is often less that in flatter, more fertile waters. The smaller forage often forces a successful angler to toss smaller baits. Tiny jigs, worms, and crankbaits can be very productive in such rocky waters.

Many mountainous reservoirs and lakes offer numerous opportunities to develop rock fishing techniques. Successful anglers may fish parallel to the bluff.

I'll systematically check out all bluff or canyon rim areas for rock slides. Often my X-16 chart recorder will reveal any underwater bar structure. All rocky foundations can hold bass, and all bear inspection. Fish the shallower ones first, and then move to deeper terrain.

Scan the shoreline for some indication of what is below and learn to 'read' the water. Knowing that big boulders often roll down a rock slide to stop near the bottom might just clue you in to where the lunkers hide. Rock outcropping above the surface can tell you a lot about what is below. So can a mask and snorkel if you have the time and inclination.

You can utilize these techniques on bodies of water from the deep, clear mountainous lakes in the west, to the Ozark-contained reservoirs in the mid-west, to the Appalachian impoundments in the east. They could result in a "rocky road" for the bass population, so, please be humble and practice conservation.

CHAPTER 10

RIVER REVELATIONS

Patterning Bass In Slowly Moving Water

WARM WATER CREEKS, bayous and rivers throughout the country vary in size and flowage, but most that are wet year around contain largemouth bass. Thousands of miles of waterways exist within a day's drive for the exploring bass angler, and river bass are often easier to pattern than those living in a lake.

A variety of water types exist, and many have given up largemouth of significant size. Water flows slowly through old river beds in some on the lower coastal plains, while in others through hill country, the current seems more conducive to white-water canoeing than to chasing after bass. The better ones for largemouth are basically slow-moving, meandering and deep.

Some tributaries are influenced by springs and drop in elevation, while the discharge of a reservoir dam or spillway may dictate the character of others. Many smaller tributaries are not known for their fishing opportunities, yet the angling can be outstanding. While some creeks and rivers run through privately-owned lands, all navigable waters are usually publicly owned.

Moving along the river or creek via a small boat or canoe is a normal mode of transportation. Navigation may present some problems, more often in the form of overhanging trees, logs and timber, rocky stretches, sandbars and other potential hazards to maneuver around. Often, the unspoiled beauty of small passageways is well worth the trip. The tremendous action normally present will make it even more memorable.

Other larger waterways also offer quiet stretches. The rate of flow varies with the fluctuating water tables and/or spillway discharge rate. The water clarity depends, in part, upon the rainfall and springs influence and the characteristics of the watershed.

Largemouth bass that inhabit moving waters are, just like their lake counterparts, structure-oriented. They seek out cover in which to live and feed. Largemouth will usually avoid high-current areas, prefering quieter water that is adjacent or below tumbling ripples. Most flowages offer numerous "holes" carved out by the currents or created by small sinkholes.

An obvious surface key to patterning bass is locating structure on the bends. Contrary to some beliefs, the depths in the creeks and streams vary greatly, depending on where you are looking. Outer bends are generally the deepest part of a waterway.

In the smaller creeks, vegetation and habitat can be limited. Often brush and fallen trees provide the only shoreline cover in tiny tributaries. The food base though is primarily small forage fish and crustacean. Crayfish frequent the rocky shoal areas and deep undercut banks. These are the better areas in any flowing water environment.

Top Techniques

Catching bass from moving waters often requires special techniques. While they may have seldom seen lures, most bass are well aware of their environment and of their accessibility to outside predation. Stealth may be of paramount importance when an angler approaches a good-looking spot. Keeping noise to an absolute minimum is usually wise in order to sneak up on the bass. Banging the canoe or boat with an oar or paddle can quickly scare off fish.

Drifting a small stream is not as easy as it sounds. In the fast stretches, you may have to paddle hard to keep the boat straight. Then once a rapid has been successfully navigated, you have to present your lure to the fish, as quickly as possible, unless you stop the craft.

A drift should consider possible anchorage and boat position. When the boat is floating toward a productive-looking pocket, plan ahead on tying up to an emergent tree trunk or anchoring in order to end up in the best position from which to cast.

Bass, like the author's 6 pounder, will move into small tributaries off of the main river channels to feed.

Determine the area from which you want to cast and identify the obstructions that you will have to cast around or under to penetrate the bass hideout. A particularly good area along the waterways is any point formed by the intersection of two tributaries. Currents create well-defined points where the greatest drop occurs. That's the spot offering the most potential holding structure for largemouth bass.

The heavy cover along the deep stretches should be worked thoroughly before moving shallower. Check out the tiny tributaries that often harbor flooded brush or weed beds. Fish slowly as you move the boat through these areas for best results. Competition for the best moving waters is seldom a problem.

A small bait that resembles the predominant forage will often catch the most fish for you. It's an opportunity for ultralight tackle, if you are so inclined. And, it's an opportunity for an angler to catch several bass.

If the waters are very clear, keep in mind that the bass have maximum visibility during high-noon. Lure selection then is critical. During low light times, tying on the "perfect" bait might not be as important. Cloudy days and the early morning and late afternoon time periods on the often overgrown creeks are more conducive to catching bass. Watching fish come apparently out of nowhere and follow the lure should peak the interest of any angler.

Hooking a couple of small bass that take to the sky and try to throw the bait is exciting. Being able to watch the battle in its entirety as the fish goes from the water to the air-medium is something that most anglers will not forget for a long time.

The upper reaches of small creeks that freshen up rivers often contain some exciting bass action. Spring fishing in such places can be rewarding since bass will sometimes move to that water to spawn. They just want to get away from all the boat traffic usually found in larger, more navigable waters.

Bass prefer habitat out of the "main stream" of activity. They like peace and quiet and protection. Shoal areas and sandbars limit boat traffic. I've often had to get out of my boat and wade past a bar to get to the deeper water on the other side.

Tributaries that lead to "nowhere" are opportunities for bass anglers. Depths may vary from a few feet to 10 or 12 and the fishing

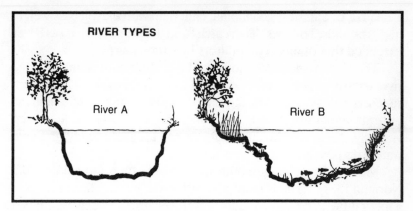

FIGURE 12 - River A exhibits little evidence of biological productivity of plants and fish. These "sterile" types of rivers should be avoided. The nutrient-rich waters depicted in river B offer obvious plant life and forage. These are the river waters that will offer healthy, active populations of bass.

will also. Many are excellent fisheries while some are not. Those with minimal water movement may become stagnant and offer few sport fish.

Lessons For Cold, Muddy River Water

With fall comes changing weather and, oft-times, extremely tough fishing conditions. High, muddy and turbulent rivers in combination with rapidly decreasing water temperatures make patterning bass a difficult challenge.

While many anglers don't fare well at all in such an environment, some seasoned fishermen are able to figure out how they can catch fish. Their productive patterns may work for the rest of us, if we are ever forced into such a situation.

Such conditions occurred a couple of winters ago at the Redman All-American Championship held on the Arkansas River in Little Rock. The late November showcase found 43 anglers from around the country mostly frustrated by the high, turbid waters that swept through the "pools" above and below Arkansas's capital city.

One man, though, figured out the harsh conditions that the river threw at him and walked away with a check for $100,000.00. O.T.

97

Fears III, of Sallisaw, Oklahoma, ended up with eleven bass weighing 28 pounds, 3 ounces. That catch from the muddy Arkansas River exceeded that of most competitors by a wide margin.

The Oklahoma professional and the other contestants saw the river drop two feet over the course of the two day event. The current speed, running rampant on day one, decreased by about 60% and the water temperature dropped by 3 degrees. The turbid water stayed virtually the same. Such conditions are tough. Muddy and cold waters do pose problems to fishermen.

Most of Fears' largemouth were caught on a tan-colored Bill Norman Deep Little N crankbait with black back. The color made a lot of difference in the muddy water, because it closely resembled the shad that are predominant in the Arkansas River, according to the former fishery biologist. Fears drew on his experience fishing the same river, far upstream in Oklahoma. He had known that river bass seem to hit that particular color better than other colors during the late fall.

He found his fish at a river jetty that had a hole in it, which allowed some current through. While the river was high and the current in the main channel was flowing strong, the bass were stacked up on the points of the hole. Fears positioned his boat below the hole and cast up-current and across the point. The water was hitting the point in such a fashion that it was boiling up on the point.

The shad were washing by those areas and the bass were aggressively feeding on them. They didn't hit the bait hard, however. They would simply grab the lure. They felt like a log. There was a break in the current on all points under water, and the fish were lying in that break. Fears brought his crankbait along the point for several of his strikes.

Fears had a second pattern that was also productive. A bank in the back of an old slough with a lot of lay-down timber also held numerous largemouth. The fish were away from the bank, out on the tips of the logs, 6 to 8 foot deep. Current swept by the slough and the bass were using the submerged trees to break the effects of the current.

The professional cast parallel to the tree and worked his crank bait down into the tree limbs. The fish would simply grab the lure as

This pair that totaled almost 17 pounds were taken from heavy cover along deep stretches of a slow-moving river.

it came over a limb. He fished the water column from 6 to 18 feet of water and caught his larger bass from the deeper water. A key to his catching larger fish, according to Fears, was the use of a 7-foot rod and cranking reel. The slow retrieve ratio reel slowed the bait down and gave fish more time to see it.

Pattern Adjustment

The strong current present on day one changed on the second day - it slowed to almost nothing. There was slack, glassy water with no ripple along the jetty. Consequently, the fish on the jetty points moved and Fears was able to catch only one 13-inch bass from that area.

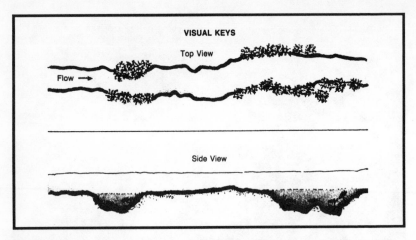

FIGURE 13 - *Treeless banks composed of sandy marsh soil usually denote shallow waters, while those shorelines with extensive tree cover reveal deeper topography. Bass often hold in the deeper waters of a river or creek.*

The fish back in the slough were likewise affected. When the current drops on a river, the bass don't have to relate to cover any longer to use as ambush points. The largemouth can move off and search for shad in open water. Since shad don't relate to structure, that's where they are most commonly found.

The water temperature was gradually falling all week, from 58 degrees early on to 53 on the final day of fishing. Fears calculated that when the river began to fall, there would be a lot of bass pulled from the flooded sloughs and creeks. Fish that are just off the river in the sloughs and creeks will pull back out into the river itself, he reasoned. So, he began looking at water temperatures in the practice rounds.

"With a dropping water temperature, the fish will generally look for the warmest water they can find. That was in the main channel of the river. The further back into a creek that you went, the colder the water would be. River bass are notorious for moving long distances, up to a mile or so. They have no problem at all when they have to move 1/4 of a mile."

The slough and jetty area that he fished had water temperatures that were very comparable to the river water temperatures. Clarity of the Arkansas didn't really matter that much, according to Fears, whose 13-year experience working for the U.S. Fish and Wildlife Service helped him become a sucessful full-time fisherman. The fish in that river were used to dingy, off-colored water.

Many anglers have caught some of their best strings of bass when the trolling motor was churning mud in one foot of cold river water. The conditions can be tough, but the bass aren't always turned off. Try them.

CHAPTER 11

FOAMING WATER FAIRS

Runoffs, Dams And Other Activity Funnels

TRYING TO FIGURE out where largemouth bass may be on a small stream blocked by a dam should be an easy task. While I will generally head to the tail waters or spillway if accessible, sometimes the better angling may be closer to the ramp. I discovered this one day when exploring the Everglades.

A small dam spread across a tributary in front of me, and the swirling water beneath the concrete structure would hold some largemouth. I knew that. I cautiously moved up toward the dam, tossing a small spinner. My third cast resulted in a smashing strike and a high flying bass. I released the 17 inch long fish and cast again.

I worked the bait near the rocky bottom knowing not only of the possible snags but also of the bass that await. A two pound largemouth struck at it, and after three leaps skyward and a good tussle in the fast current, it was brought aboard. In the following ten minutes, I caught another four more largemouth and missed a couple of good strikes. The action below the dam slowed, though, and I began thinking of an alternate pattern that might work on additional bass.

My boat was anchored about 30 feet from the dam structure. The bottom became shallower toward the dam, reaching near the surface in a couple of areas. I had thoroughly worked most of the water in the spillway with a variety of lures, and it was time to try a new area, like the productive-looking cover on the shore just above the dam. The surface of the water was about eye-level and I had no idea how deep it was on the other side, but it was worth losing a lure to find out!

I tossed a Little George as far as I could along the shoreline above the dam. I half-way expected a hang-up before my retrieve had reached the dam and surely anticipated hooking the top of the dam if the lure got that far.

The heavy tail-spinner lure was about 20 feet from the dam's lip when my rod was jolted by the sudden attack of a hungry largemouth. The three pounder jumped twice before I worked her to the dam. The third time I saw her was when I horsed her over the dam. She fell six feet down into the white water as I frantically reeled to take up the event's resulting slack. I gained control again and led her out of the rocks and to the boat.

I netted her and cast again. My next three casts were unproductive, but I did get my lure to scoot across the dam without a hang-up. The fourth cast attracted another strike, however, and a two pound bass was soon tumbling over the dam. The lure was dislodged in the fall, and the bass was in a new territory.

In the following hour, I caught three more "dare-devil" bass. My catch from the formidable obstacle was sizable, yet I had only lost one lure in the rocks below the dam and one to a snag above the structure. The ease with which the lure and hooked bass could be brought over the dam was surprising. While the great angling opportunity that exists in such places is passed over by the average caster, I learned to fish both side of the structure!

In addition to a food source, productive running water areas like the spillway and dam structure must also have the important ingredients of depth and cover. Adequate amounts of each is required to hold fish for extended periods. Depths of over 3 feet in roily water and some nearby structure should also be present for optimal conditions.

Moving water is a natural attraction to largemouth and most other game fish. Quite a few anglers concentrate on the advantages of the flow. Locating such conditions and then fishing the currents is becoming increasingly popular. While moving water is generally rich in nutrients, it is also usually cooler and more oxygenated.

With the abundant food supply, the fish won't have to expend much energy chasing after smaller members of the food chain. The result is larger fish in such locations. When they have first shot at the

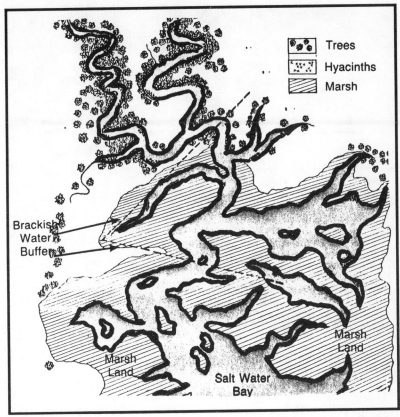

FIGURE 14 - While oxygen levels may be extremely low in some areas, they will always be higher where the water is moving, such as in tidewaters. Numerous cuts along the bank usually exist and are great

supply, why wouldn't they grow faster and bigger. Baitfish are often washed into the mouths of their prey, and while it is not always possible to find "foaming water", when you can locate some, you'll probably catch some fish.

Turbulent waters are also often tough to fish. They require appropriate techniques dependent upon the cover that is available. The lure chosen must be presented properly to assure action, even in fish-laden waters. In some areas, the only slack water will be right against shore or in a deep water pool below turbulent outflow

Largemouth will often lie at the edge of the heavy current in quieter surroundings. They will position themselves near an oft times abundant food supply.

current. Drift with the current, and you may miss many potential hot spots. Use your electric trolling motor to hold against the current, and you'll probably catch some bass.

For more prime action, move to the outside of the first bend downstream of the runout or dam tailrace where the current is strongest. This is where debris and other log jams form, and it is the area that should be fished from the inner bend. Bass hold in such areas to await the forage washing by.

Another productive ploy is to find an area that geographically narrows down while current speeds up. This provides a great ambush point for bass just below the "neck". Tributaries which also carry runoff of some sort are prime bass hot spots. Water movement and depth are requirements of the better tributary areas.

Fringe Elements

Many such tributaries contain springs that bring waters low in pH. They will be basic (above 7.0 pH or higher), versus acid, but they'll be somewhere between 7.2 to 7.4, according to Dick Healey, President of Lake Systems. Such waters coming into an area with dense vegetation and high corresponding photosynthesis will often form an "edge" which will hold fish like a magnet.

"I've seen numerous cases where I would launch a boat and find the pH in the high 9's due to an algae bloom," says Healey. "Then a half mile or so away, I've found the pH around 7. So why the difference? Because probably, there is a spring or secondary feeder creek bringing buffered water into that second area.

To effectively fish such areas, cast a lure up against any bank with cover in the form of rocks or brush. These areas on the fringe of moving water can hold some big bass. Cast to any protruding cover in the current where the fish may lie behind the force breaker. Bass prefer not to have to continually fight the swift waters and will usually be on the outside edge of a current force.

A strong trolling motor will aid in precisely controlling a drift, but be prepared for sudden changes in current direction which may sweep a craft into shore. Try to position the boat in eddies or out of the current, so that control time will be minimal. Boat control in moving waters is important when you are not anchored.

Prime Turbulent Patterns

Some of the better bass hangouts deserve special attention and appropriate lure presentations. Four great areas are those mentioned below.

1. A good area for finding bass concentrations is beneath the foam. Many impoundments in the state have spillways, and often the smaller reservoirs have low-water dams which offer the agitated water beneath. Dam tailrace waters are excellent locations to cast small crankbaits, spoons, and weighted plastic worms.

The best retrieve for tailrace waters is one that allows the lure to bump the bottom structure. Rocks, logs and other debris concentrate bass in such areas, and a lure that bumps them will provoke strikes. When oxygen levels may be extremely low in some parts of

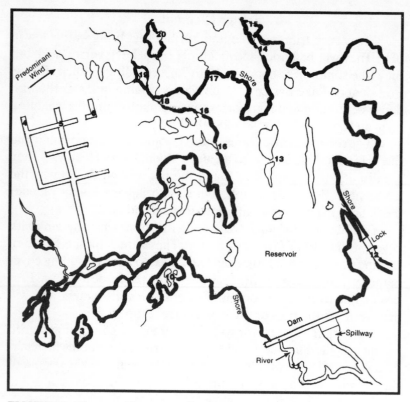

FIGURE 15 - There are 20 cuts, runoffs and other potential water infusion areas on this typical lake. Can you determine why each may be productive and when?

a lake, they will normally be higher where the water is moving. The pH value and temperature levels are often ideal also for optimal results.

2. Water level control structures holding back a creek, a levee marsh or man-dug waters are prime areas to find bass foraging on morsels washing down. Such places have a small outlet where water leaves one compartment or marsh area and flows out into a canal, creek or another compartment. Largemouth will often lie at the edge of the heavy current in quieter surroundings. Small hollow grub baits are productive in such spots. The forage base is often smaller in the smaller waters, so the little baits may work better here.

Position the boat downstream from the control structure and cast to the side of it near the shore. Allow the lure to drop off the edge of the cover and tumble to the bottom. Keep a careful eye on the bait as it bumps along the bottom toward you, and set the hook if the line jumps. Several casts may be needed to entice the first bass to hit, or you may locate a hungry concentration of largemouth on the initial cast to the structure.

3. Rains insure a continuing supply of fresh foods washing downstream. Runoff areas where a small creek bed fills up fast or where a lake cove necks down providing a current are great places for largemouth. In colder weather when bass don't like to move far for anything, the fresh food supply will be washing by in front of them. Highly visible baits, such as chrome-plated crankbaits, silver vibrating plugs and other colorful "active" lures can be successful here. Cast beyond the point where the runoff enters, if possible, and bring the lure out of the murky water into the clearer waters. Bass will normally wait there for a chance at forage washing by.

4. Moving water at the mouths of cuts or inlets or around islands usually provides bass with essentials of forage, depth and cover. The smart angler will be right there casting and probably, filling a stringer. Some slower baits like the Texas-rigged worms and topwater minnow plugs produce in these places.

Bass Behavior

Largemouth normally face the current awaiting forage to wash down toward them. Any forage imitation moving "upstream" against the current will seldom result in a strike. The bogus bait appears unnatural to the wary largemouth emphasizing that lure presentation in these situations is critical.

A lure tossed into fast moving water may be difficult to control and strikes difficult to detect. Protected waters off the main current in eddies are prime areas to work for largemouth. Cast your lure up current and bring it back across the eddy line. It is at the "edge" of fast water where most strikes will occur.

Oxbow areas just below a dam are ideal spots for turbulent water largemouth. Hungry largemouth lie out of the fast current in quiet waters on the edge. When water intensity coming over a dam

After a shower has passed, ditches and ravines in flat country offer bass a continuing supply of fresh foods washing downstream. Cuts where a small creek empties into a river or lake provide a current and largemouth.

subsides, fishing may be off. Bass hiding behind the shallow spots and in the oxbow away from main river current may relocate. Often, they will move back up beneath the froth at the base of the dam.

The successful angler in the dam's spillway should be a line watcher. Due to water turbulence, a careful eye on the monofilament is vital. I like Berkley Tri-Max photochromatic line which offers great visibility above water for better line control, yet virtually disappears in the water. It is limp enough for easy casting, yet is tough enough to drag a jiggin spoon along a sandy bottom below a spillway. My line weights vary from 14 pound test up to 20 for normal moving-water situations.

Lure Selection

Bass in foaming waters have little time to critically analyze the line or to detect a counterfeit bait. Lure selection is, however, very important to the successful angler with aspirations toward catching several largemouth.

Crankbaits are excellent choices for use in turbulent waters and Norman's Big "N" series in a shad paint job is my favorite selection for such areas. I'll always lean toward a shad or crayfish imitation in these forage-intensive places. Chrome sides and brown crayfish patterns that run five to ten feet down take their share of largemouth cranked from beneath swirling water.

Tail-spinner baits and weedless Texas-rigged worms also attract their share in these fishy areas. My favorite plastic wiggler is a seven-inch curly-tail model in motor oil or brown. Earth-tone colors usually resemble snakes that swim about on water, and they are good selections.

Lures that get down quick in the turbulent water and resemble forage are hard to beat. The bass are in the swirling environment waiting for the properly presented bait.

CHAPTER 12

OPEN WATER ROAMING

Following Shad Schools To Better Fishing

THE MOST REWARDING bass fishing action of your life will probably be when a school of largemouth erupts beside your boat some day. It's a feeding frenzy that you won't want to miss. The object of the bass appetite is most commonly the morsel called threadfin shad.

They probably inhabitat waters near you. Threadfin range from Guatemala and Belize in Central America, north to Ohio and Pennsylvania, and from Florida west along the Gulf coast drainage to California. Oklahoma, Tennessee, Arizona and even Hawaii have populations of threadfin, so they're not just a southern forage fish. Additionally, they inhabit power plant (heated) waters further north of their common range.

The factor that limits their range depends, of course, on their vulnerability to winter kill. Biologists have found that shad mortality starts at about 44 degrees F in the southern states, while an acclimated shad population in a northern lake may tolerate slightly lower temperatures. Largemouth, of course, prefer them alive.

Bass don't feel much like feeding in cold temperatures, but when things warm up a bit, the threadfin forage will be needed badly. Some studies have found that bass in midwestern reservoirs prefer a diet of only shad in the winter. Stomach analyses have also revealed that bass can consume three or four percent of their body weight each day in shad. A ten-pounder will eat a bunch!

Since shad are susceptible to cold water, this has the effect of concentrating the fish where the water is warmest during winter

An angler should always be alert for gull activity, which could reveal schools of bass below. Following on the trail of sea gulls and shad schools roving about the lake can be exciting.

months. That provides the largemouth with easy pickins. The shad move into the heated discharge waters of many power plant reservoirs, for example, and that will make feeding easier for them.

As a baitfish, little rivals the threadfin shad. They only grow to a few inches and are a more manageable shad than their cousin, the gizzard shad. The threadfin thrive in huge schools which abound in most of the country's southern reservoirs and lakes. Those are often "forage flotillas" for ever-hungry largemouth bass.

The threadfin's sensitivity to cold temperature is important to the angler; that fact helps him to locate a school of shad and a nearby school of hungry bass through the aid of either a water temperature

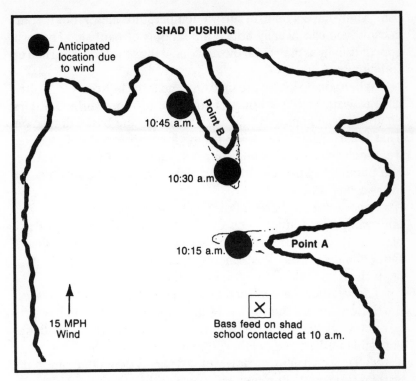

FIGURE 16 - *Plankton will drift toward shore with a steady wind, so the threadfin can be found in shallow waters at times. The wind and wave action will also filter the sun's rays and shallower running lures may be more productive under such circumstances. The wave action will pile up the schools of shad on shallow points and bass simply move up from the deep after them. High winds push them near, and sometimes onto, the shoreline.*

meter, Multi-C-Lector or a chart recorder (depth finder). Just how to use those tools to find the schoolers is important.

The water temperature meter provides surface or depth readouts when a probe is lowered over the side. The Multi-C-Lector provides a digital readout of the water temperature at different depths, as the probe automatically lowers. It also reveals other water chemistry characteristics important to the presence of both shad and bass.

The depth finder, LCD unit or chart recorder, can be essential in a successful search for schooling bass and their favorite forage fish. Many have a built-in surface temperature meter, but if yours doesn't, you can usually notice the schools of baitfish. They will appear usually as masses on the readout, if the sensitivity is turned up sufficiently.

When you do locate the shad on or near the bottom, you'll often have to wait for a few hours of sunshine to warm surface waters. Shad will usually move to the surface before the bass will turn on. That is particularly true when fishing for schoolers during late fall weather, which is often chilly for a straight week. Air temperatures that plummet to the low 30's each night will drive the shad deeper into warmer water.

I once was on a Texas power plant reservoir and came across an interesting old 40-foot deep creek channel. Thousands of fish blackened my chart recorder just above the bottom contour line of the cooling reservoir. Vast schools of threadfin covered the 10-foot deep channel banks from one side to the other.

The weather was cool, and I was expecting the shad to move off the bottom toward the surface by mid-morning as the sun began to warm the upper layers of water. Winter kill of the shad was negligible in the power plant reservoir due to its heated discharge water. The baitfish were, however, extremely dependent upon the warm water source during the cooler months.

That morning was colder than most and a heavy fog insulated the surface water from the warm sun rays until late in the morning. Then, around 1 p.m., the shad schools began to move toward the surface. First a few would come up, and then several would head toward the warming surface water. Streaks showing the upward movement of the baitfish were burnt into the chart paper.

Soon, larger individual fish were showing up on the chart recorder at a position about 15 feet below the newly-formed shad schools near the lake's surface. Gradually, the majority of the shad were on the surface and several bass began feeding at around 15 to 20 feet deep on the strays that were making their way up to the school. I managed to catch several nice largemouth - the biggest around 3 1/2 pounds.

There are plenty of other ways to catch bass that often follow the shad schools. Since shad are an open water species, your search for

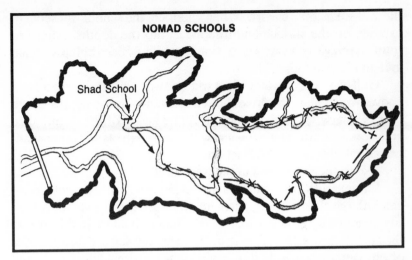

FIGURE 17 - Schooling bass often chase shad, which in their nomad ways, rove the channels and feed on plankton and insect larvae. The forage fish are usually concentrated within five feet of the lake's surface while feeding, since sunlight promotes the growth of the plankton. The shad usually avoid heavy cover, since bass may be waiting in ambush. They move into open water, but school bass still follow.

the largemouth that forage on them should begin there. Some of the following patterns may help put a few more in your boat, when you do come across a bass feeding frenzy.

1. Fish near-surface water over river channels

Schooling bass often chase shad, which in their nomad ways, rove the channels and feed on plankton and insect larvae. The forage fish are usually concentrated within five feet of the lake's surface while feeding, since sunlight promotes the growth of the plankton. The water temperature has to be tolerable, of course, for them to be at the surface.

At times, huge schools of bass can be seen feeding on the shad schools right on the surface. On a calm lake, their presence can hardly go undetected. The shad usually avoid heavy cover, since bass may be waiting in ambush. They move into open water, but school bass still follow.

2. Fish beneath the birds

The little two to three-inch threadfin will make small ripples on the surface as they cavort. When spooked, the school will seem to explode on the surface and disappear into the depths, usually to return a few yards away. This action is usually noticed by birds, which love to feed on these fish.

Gulls and other water birds will be swooping at the shad from above, which may just drive the schools down to the depths of the bass. Otherwise, the largemouth will be aware of the disturbance and move upward. Smart anglers will toss crankbaits and other shad-imitations around any bird action.

3. Fish the frenzy and in the wake of it

Largemouth bass can usually be found 12 to 25 feet down, beneath the shad schools, and when they get the urge to feed, they simply move up. They will drive the shad into an excited frenzy as they try to escape the slashing bass. Dramatic surface disturbances often occur as the bass boil and swirl in the baitfish schools, knocking several shad into the air. Largemouth will hit almost any lure resembling a shad while in the "kill everything that moves" mode.

The bass will feed until they're full, then cough up some and go for more. Maimed and crippled shad are left on the surface in the wake of the disaster as the remainder of the school flees in panic. The wounded members of the shad tribe that escape the bass feeding mayhem may end up in the mouth of a trailing bass or on a fatal flight with an awaiting bird.

4. Look for gull "inaction" to tip off a location

The gull, like the bass, is never far away from the schools of shad. The gulls can spot the deeper shad schools easily from the air on a sunny day, and knowing where the gulls are can certainly help an angler to pinpoint the forage and the schooling bass.

From fall through the first part of spring, finding the area of the lake where the gulls are working or just resting is important. The resting gulls will usually be sitting over the schools of shad, waiting for bass to start feeding from below, thereby driving them up.

5. Fish the underwater paths

Bass will herd these schools of shad around the lake, periodically slashing at them and turning the surface water into foam. They'll attack the shad near submerged creek or river channel beds, near the edges of flooded timber stands, in boat lanes through heavy vegeta-

118

It's often easy to catch a bunch from schooling bass, but to catch larger ones, you must get your lure to descend into the depths beneath the smaller fish.

tion or cover and on underwater islands or 'humps' on the lake bottom. They will wait in nearby cover for these schools to wander along defined paths, and then pop them.

Shad will use the submerged creek channels and boat lanes to travel around the lake. They will try to stay away from their predators at the edge of the timber, but it is not always easy. They will travel the underwater paths, which may also lead them through bridges, where they are again an easier target for the largemouth.

6. Fish suspended school bass beneath the shad

In such 'tight quarters', the shad are mighty uneasy and very spooky. And justly so, because once the bass have attacked one school, they'll simply retreat to their hideaway and wait for the next

119

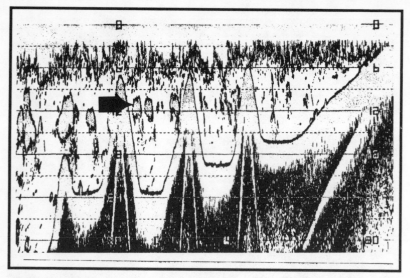

FIGURE 18 - Schools of baitfish, such as threadfin shad, can sometimes be noticed on the chart recorder moving down a submerged river channel.

one to amble past. In more open water, however, the bass may simply fall back to a suspended position just below the feeding zone and wait for another school of shad to meander by. An angler can often fish deep-running baits beneath the baitfish for bass action.

7. Have heavy lures ready

At times, schooling activity can be great for the angler, but in many cases the shad and bass will 'sound' before the angler reaches them. The latter is probably the rule on many waters. Some places always seem to have schooling activity, but seldom do the fishermen connect.

Bass will chase shad all over the place, but unless your lure hits near a breaking fish, forget about fried fillets. It takes too long to switch lures for schooling activity, so an angler needs to have handy a rod rigged with a heavy shad-like lure. A tail spinner lure or heavy crankbait is ideal for those 150-foot casts that may be required to hit a breaking school of fish.

8. Fish the tributary inlets and river bends

The shad are usually corralled by bass in the river near bends and

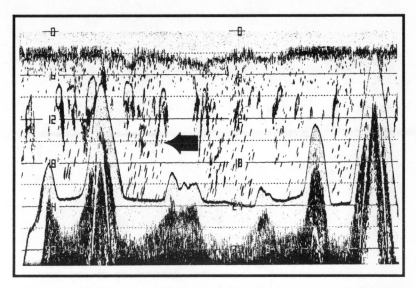

FIGURE 19 - Bass may be scattered beneath the baitfish schools, so getting your lure down to them should result in numerous strikes. Notice the larger fish beneath the forage "clouds."

at creek inlets. I've found that the most successful way to cash in on the action is to sit in the middle of the inlet and fish the drops, down into deep water. A shad imitation fished along the river bottom in deep water can lure some of the up-and-down bass to the stringer. The drops are always present where surface activity exists, since the bass would not be able to attack the shad schools so easily in open water.

9. Match the lure size and color to the forage

For best results, match the lure size to the size of shad that the bass are feeding on. To stimulate bass action, the lure should be worked slowly beneath the area where the surface activity had occurred. If you can't catch the eager school bass while they are slaughtering the defenseless shad on top, keep your patience and try them deep.

10. Let the wind point you in the right direction

Shad will, of course, follow drifting plankton to feed and bass won't be far behind as the next step in the food chain. Plankton will

FIGURE 20 - Shad will move around the open water and not attract the attention of bass...for awhile. Then, a few largemouth will show up, and move the baitfish toward the surface.

drift toward shore with a steady wind, so the threadfin can be found in shallow waters at times. Thus, the windward shore is a place to begin your search for schooling largemouth.

The wind and wave action will also filter the sun's rays and allow the shad to feed nearer the surface than normal. Since the water clarity and light rays are determining factors in how deep the shad will be, wave action is just what the bass angler needs also. Shallower running lures may be more productive under such circumstances.

11. Fish waves that are breaking across points

The wave action will pile up the schools of shad on shallow points and bass simply move up from the deep after them. The mass of the shad schools is such that their location is highly dependent on wind conditions. High winds push them near, and sometimes onto, the shoreline. The lower light penetration brings them closer to the surface to feed, and game fish follow suit.

12 Follow the currents through a lake or reservoir

Plankton and minute organic matter drifts not only with the wind, but also with the current. Due to its light weight, the matter is normally found near the surface. Shad will move in such currents to feed and again, bass will follow the forage. Current sweeps through bridges, along submerged creek channels and even in unsuspecting places on a lake. The current in heated discharge waters from power plants almost always has an abundance of threadfin shad.

Both shad and bass will normally face into the current while feeding, but an angler can often determine a slight current by noting in which direction the schools of shad are traveling. The current in some reservoirs fluctuates according to whether the turbines at the dam are running or not. Lake drawdowns and even navigational lock use can affect a current in some lakes, and this will many times trigger bass into a feeding spree on the hapless shad.

Those are some of the ways to boost a stringer when around schooling bass. Never take more than you can eat and leave some for me, regardless of the time of year. The occurrence of surface action may be more prominent in the summer months in many lakes, but some waters produce such activity any month with little wind and warm surface water.

CHAPTER 13

WICKED WIND AND WEATHER

Winning Ways To Combat Head Winds

THE 200-ACRE LAKE was dead calm. The threatening skies in the north were approaching due to winds at high altitude. The front line of clouds had blocked the sun's rays as we arrived at the lake. It was literally the calm before the storm.

My brother Ron and I had trailered his boat to the small lake that morning, but when we left his house at about 8 a.m. the skies were clear. We decided to launch the boat at any rate and keep our rain suits handy. We had come to fish. A two minute boat ride put us at a small dam and we started tossing plugs.

We quickly established a pattern. On my fifth cast with a Big N crankbait, I put my second fish in the boat and Ron had added one to the live well also. In the next 20 minutes as the front continued to threaten our fishing, we added ten more bass to the live well. The rip-rap along the dam yielded these fish to our shad-colored crank baits. In that time, the wind had picked up and the storm was about to make its ominous presence felt.

The sky had turned black, and the white caps grew on the lake surface as the wind began to howl. We debated whether to return to the ramp and possibly beat the impending rain or rough it out on the water. We put on our rain suits and decided we'd keep fishing our quickly-found pattern as long as there was no lightning. Maybe the winds wouldn't become overpowering.

The chill hit with the first big gusts of wind and the temperature dropped about five degrees immediately. We continued to fish but had no action for the next few minutes while the rain fell. When the rain and wind finally abated, Ron nosed the boat parallel to the dam and my third cast was pounced on by a scrappy three pounder. The sky remained black, but the rain had quit. Fortunately, the bass along the rip-rap hadn't quit and we were able to capture six more chunky largemouth.

The four hour fishing trip was one of my best, and even though we entertained thoughts of turning around at the ramp without launching the boat, we had endured and it was worth it. The threatening skies, high wind and pouring rain hadn't dampened our spirits. With such a strong pattern of action, it's easy to hang in there.

In similar circumstances, I'll remember that and other productive days. As I remember, almost every time that I've been angling prior to a front, something significant has happened. I've caught huge fish (lost some too) or caught large concentrations of bass, and I've learned something valuable each time that I've fished the mess preceding a frontal system.

Fall and winter weather can be unpredictable, and 'northers' may frequently blow through the area. The fronts don't have to scare an angler if he learns to safely reap its benefits -- the good fishing. The tail end of the good weather and the time just at the beginning of the passage can be productive. After the clouds and rain have blown through leaving clear blue skies, the fisherman may as well hang up his rods.

After the front has passed, a productive pattern will be hard to come by. Very few fish will be caught. The severity of the front determines whether there is any hope at all for catching a couple of bass. A real frigid front will cool water temperatures quickly and this action will slow the fish's metabolism, slowing down their feeding movements also.

Heavy rainfall may lower the pH values to intolerable levels and drive bass deeper. High winds accompanying the rains may disperse and 'mix' the waters. Values of pH between 6.5 and 8.5 are suitable for finding some feeding bass. An approaching front with rain but little wind might trigger a feeding spree too that would last for three or four hours.

Regardless of whether the bass are hitting or not, an angler has to use the utmost care during inclement weather. A boater should

Ron Larsen braves the wind to land a 7 pounder. Big bass often prowl the shallows in stiff winds.

not only have the proper rig to handle rough weather, but he should be very knowledgeable and experienced in handling his boat and motor.

Smaller rigs have no business on the water during rough weather. Larger bass boats also are limited in the kind of 'seas' they can handle. I've seen lakes come up and swallow big rigs. Four to six foot waves on flatland lakes are not that uncommon.

A storm can bring blowing rain in so fast that boaters have no chance to reach safety. The angler should be very careful and be near some protection if he thinks a storm may blow through. I've seen at least a dozen boats sunk because their skippers lacked respect for the waters they were on and the impending weather.

Since most of the bad lightning is on the edge of a storm, the time to outrun a storm is when you first see it. After it's well on you, ride it out. Don't do what I saw a couple of fishermen do, however. As every boat headed to shore, they tied to a huge cypress tree away from other smaller trees to ride out the storm. Avoid those natural lightning attractors.

Most lightning accompanies afternoon showers, according to national statistics. It is also more common through hotter months. Since many outdoorsmen are among the injured or killed, it's important to keep abreast of the weather.

During the moist weather pattern of an approaching front, a top water pattern can be very productive. An excellent surface lure to toss in any weather variation is a clattering-type buzz bait. The metal blades are most effective at keeping the lure on the surface in an ultra slow retrieve. And that's what is needed to catch these fish. The action and the 'squeaky' sound it makes coming across the surface are keys to the success of the lure.

Once the top water pattern becomes unproductive, and the front is in, then I head for deeper water and use deep running lures. My baits are usually slower and presented deeper than at any other time. Crankbaits, like Norman's Deep Big N and DD-22, can be worked effectively in areas holding the fish.

I work the creek and river branches off lakes or larger rivers with crank baits and worms, but the fishing is usually tough. A six- or seven-inch Texas-rigged worm makes an excellent worm rig. I'll toss a Berkley Power Worm when searching for the lock-jawed bass after the front has passed.

'Ultra' light equipment may be required to seduce any bass. If the front has dropped air temperatures by several degrees, light line and small rod and reel combos definitely have their place then. Smaller-sized spinning reels loaded with eight or ten pound test monofilament is my choice for these conditions.

This abrupt change can sometimes kill fishing. The bluebird skies and windy days usually associated with a front will result in little feeding activity. The movements will likely be deep and short lived.

Since bass are cold blooded animals they cannot adapt to fluctuating weather patterns easily. They alter their daily feeding patterns

A few 10 pounders like this one from a wind-blown pattern is what excites the author. Most anglers, too, would be happy with such a catch.

to 'adjust.' They require less food when the water cools since their digestive system works slower. After the front has arrived, bass feeding becomes less frequent to maintain their existence.

The bass will move deep and stay there unless gale-force winds or rainy overcast skies return. They'll then move shallow and be easier to pattern for the average bassman. Bass feed in cool weather, but usually after a few days of consistent conditions. Learning how to make the best of changes in the weather is a must to develop a pattern, unless you can live with a limited number of trips and somewhat limited catches.

Seeing the weather conditions change is worth little to an angler that can't adjust his methods to be productive under existing conditions. Analyzing the weather to determine the best approach, his tackle, etc., is a must. If heavy cloud cover or rain exists, we can be safe in assuming that the visibility will allow you to use heavier tackle in shallower areas than you might normally try.

Wave turbulence caused by a howling wind can be good to the fishing and the lake. On a round-shaped lake, winds from any direction can be beneficial by 'stirring' up the lake into a more homogeneous body. Pockets of dead water can seldom be found in a shallow lake.

Regardless of whether we prefer to fish protected waters or not, the fact remains that the healthier lakes generally have little protection from the wind. Since frontal passages mean wind and showers, how do they relate to each other? As the weather starts to cool, so do the shallows, particularly the leeward shores. As the water temperature drops, bass will begin to move deeper.

Bass in shallow water are very susceptible to cold fronts. I've often seen unstable weather conditions drive bass to deeper water as a front moves in and drops the surface temperature several degrees. When it stabilizes at a warmer temperature, they'll move back into cover in the shallows.

The wind and rain both 'disturb' shallow waters, but that may be what the bass are waiting for. The only consistent way to catch fish during unstable weather, though, is by fishing the drops. The larger bass there are hungry and less affected by frontal movements.

Frontal bass may be very finicky and moody. Live bait is good at times when artificials won't produce. Large shiners, bullhead minnows, crayfish (if available) and other bass favorites can sometimes save a day after a cool front has pushed through.

Artificials worked slow can also produce, particularly during rain showers not associated with a real cold front. The first day of a two-day rainy period can be fantastic for the stringer. Foraging large-mouth may move into the shallows on a feeding binge that will last for a while. Showers don't have to keep you home from the lake.

A fisherman should analyze the conditions and make a good judgment as to whether or not the bass will continue to feed, and if so, on what. He should check out the potential patterns, and keep his eye out for the rain and winds that a front can bring. I usually keep my storm suit handy, while I search for bass that may prowl the shallows, even when strong winds aren't apparent.

While fishing a small reservoir, my partner and I had put two small bass in the boat in five hours of fruitless casting. The wind was minimal, only slightly disturbing the water surface. Without warning, though, a bank of clouds appeared and the wind suddenly changed, blowing from the west. The scattered clouds moving in and gusting winds of 25 miles per hour changed our stringer drastically also.

"Do you get seasick easily?" I asked my companion. "Nope," he said, wondering what I was up to I'm sure.

With that confirmation I cranked up the outboard and motored across the flats to a sandy point that the white caps were pouncing on. The boat heaved and the trolling motor changed tunes frequently as the waves tossed us about. As hard as the boat was to control under those conditions, we managed to take four nice largemouth from that point. They ranged from three to six and a half pounds. The pattern was one I had discovered before on several similar occasions.

It took extra heavy 1/2 ounce slip sinkers to get our Texas-rigged worms down to the fish, but our two hours of fighting the wind was well worth it. At the boat ramp, most fishermen we talked to had been skunked in the wind-protected areas of the reservoir. The waves acted as a filter to block out the sun's rays and to cut down on the fish's ability to see above the water, and thus the reason for our success.

Periodic winds are a reality. We must either learn to develop some effective patterns for catching bass in them, or fish only on the week days, which we all know are windless!

CHAPTER 14

TRANSITIONAL TEASING

Strategies For The Seasonal Changes

EACH YEAR, AN OCCURRENCE takes place that substantially affects our bass fishing. The occurrence is often subtle, yet it can be abrupt. It is a change of season - from winter to spring.

Weather changes are the key to determining the occurrence, not the "official" calendar notation of the arrival of spring. Bass can't read the calendar, but they can, and do, react to the change of the winter season to spring. To be productive, an angler must also change his tactics to find different patterns.

The effects are often physical as well as operational for the bass. Sows become ripe with spawn and begin to think in terms of having a family. Buck bass know their chore and set out to do the construction work on the beds - when the time seems right.

Before the spawning process takes place however, bass go through a transition phase. At this time, they can be difficult to catch. When that will occur is difficult to predict. Spring arrives at different times, depending on where in the United States the water is located.

Certain techniques can be effectively used to catch largemouth during this transitional time. Bass fishing professionals, guides and other good anglers that spend a great deal of time on the water have often figured out a pattern that works then. Information regarding the important factors to consider during this period should help the vast majority that seem to have difficulty at this time of year.

The key to successful spring fishing is the existing water temperature more than ambient temperature, according to bass professional, Ken Cook. If the water temperature is increasing, bass activity is greatly enhanced. If it is declining, activity is poorer.

"If the temperature is 52 degrees today and was 50 yesterday, then fishing should be good," he says. "If it is 52 degrees today and was 54 yesterday, then fishing won't be as good. For the best big bass action, I prefer a cloudy (showers possible) day just prior to a cold front, after several warming days."

"Until the water temperature gets around 50 to 52 degrees F, I'll usually use baits that are 'inactive,' like grubs, jigs, etc." he says. "After 52 degrees F, I'll switch to spinner baits, crankbaits, minnow type baits. They'll cause more reaction strikes since bass are much more active."

Cook will switch to larger baits then like the jig-n-pig since some crayfish become very active about 52 degrees F. This varies somewhat with latitude and species of crayfish, according to the pro.

Specific activity of bass also may vary with their acclimatization, according to the former fishery biologist. Bass in Oklahoma or Texas are not very active until the temperature reaches 50 degrees, but bass in more northern latitudes are usually much more active at 47 to 50 degrees F.

"Good baits to use should usually resemble crayfish," says Cook. "They are the most preferred food at this time because of their ease of capture and high protein level. Flashy spinnerbaits which imitate big shad and provide a big bite are also excellent."

Usually the first water to warm up after the winter cold periods is in the northeast part of a lake, especially if this is the upper reaches of the lake, according to Cook. This is caused by rapid warming of substrata by a south latitude sun in the spring. Cook looks for such areas of warmer water and concentrates angling activities there.

Other productive bass anglers will also search for a distinguishable thermal difference in their bass waters. During the first few weeks of spring, bass still want deep water around or close by, so that when a front blows in, he can move back into the deeper water. Look for shallow flats or a series of shallow ridges with a channel or ditch nearby.

A definite approach to pre-Spring fishing is required for consistent success. An Arkie jig with a Berkley Strike Rind strip is

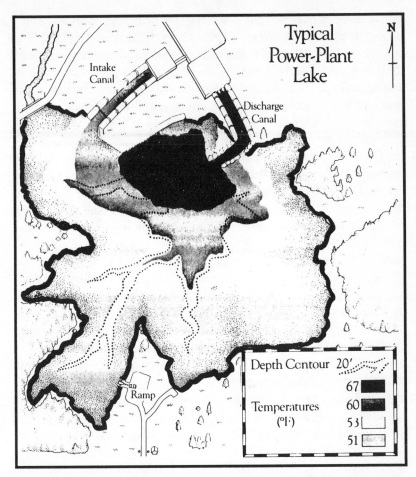

FIGURE 21 - Power plant waters are not as easily affected by cold fronts as are other shallow, natural lakes. Areas around the discharge will be the warmest water, which attract forage and bass.

productive in the water that's still cold, but it requires a slow approach. The jig can be worked easily in and out of cover, teasing a possibly inactive fish. Two other lures that are effective under such conditions are a large single blade spinner bait and a slow wobbling Norman crankbait. Hard baits also work well with the slow retrieve.

The timing key to moving to shallower water is often determined

135

by the number of consecutive warm days and nights. Bass will lunch on the nearest shallow hump before dispersing into the flats. The continued warm days and nights send the largemouth roving into shallow water. Lures change then, and the productive pattern angler will be covering a lot of water and moving often. Spinners and cranks may be the bread and butter now, but a jig-and-pork combo will still produce the better fish.

Such an approach works on deeper waters as well. With slightly longer days, warming weather and rising water, the smart deep reservoir angler moves shallow and fishes spinnerbaits in any newly flooded cover that he can find. He'll also search out good "flippin' bites" in pockets of heavy cover and some floating debris.

After a stretch of warm sunny days, look to the coves on the north side of the lake, as they warm up the quickest. They need to be shallow bays that are protected from the wind, especially the closer it gets to spring. The key areas to check in early spring are the secondary points in those bays. Those are the places you'll find the big females which have moved from the outside points.

The whole spring movement can often be watched on the graph. As the weather warms, you can watch the baitfish come up from very deep water to maybe 10 or 15 feet. But as soon as a front comes by, it pushes them right back down!

Texas bass pro, Tommy Martin looks at several factors or signs to determine just when to go to his spring patterns. They are:

1. A rise in water temperature during the middle of the day, e.g. 11 a.m. to sunset;

2. Bass movement in the shallows during the midday, i.e. bass chasing baitfish, etc.;

3. When he can no longer catch bass in the deep water areas that they winter in.

He'll then try to find the largemouth in the shallow water spawning areas.

"When the surface temperature starts to warm, the bass head toward shallow water and their spawning grounds," says Martin. "Normally the better fishing will happen from 11 a.m. to dark. This is when the water will get the warmest and causes the bass to be more active."

A warm, sunny morning is one that creates a winter fog and active bass. The larger, less affected largemouth will be the most active fish, however, so fish deep for them.

When looking for early spring bass, Martin looks for coves, bays and pockets that are protected from north winds. These waters, as we have noted, will warm up the quickest and the bass will usually become active here first. A good temperature gauge is a must for spring fishing, according to the professional.

"Your water temperature can change as much as 10 degrees from the main lake water to the back of the coves, bays and pockets," he explains. "The bass will become active first, of course, in the warmest water."

A variety of patterns (techniques and lures) work well for Martin during the transition from winter to early spring. Crankbaits such as the Bomber Model 7A, Norman Deep Little N, Rattletraps and

Hotspots in crawfish or shad patterns are productive then in five to 15 feet of water.

A 1/2 oz. spinnerbait is a favorite of Martin's. He prefers one with a single copper or gold, No.5 willow leaf blade and a white, chartreuse or white/yellow skirt. He'll fish the single willow leaf spinnerbait slowly two or three feet under the water or maybe even bumping shallow bottom. Very rarely will Martin fish a spinnerbait in water deeper than 7 feet.

"I catch most of my larger bass on a jig and lizard," says Martin. "I use a somewhat lighter jig than I would use during the winter months when I am fishing deep. I use a 3/16 oz., 5/16 oz. and a 1/2 oz. depending on the actual water depth and the amount of cover I am fishing. I prefer a brown jig with brown or black spring lizard, or a black/blue jig with black lizard."

"The minnow imitation lure can also be a real killer this time of the year if the conditions are right," stresses Martin. "A Bomber Long A is especially effective in calm water during the middle of the day when the water is warmest. Fish it around heavy cover in the backs of coves and on the flats in one to five feet of water."

Martin's favorite color is gold with an orange belly, and his favorite technique is to cast the lure close to cover and just let it sit until the rings have disappeared. He'll then very lightly twitch the lure, let it set a few more seconds and then twitch it again.

"If you haven't gotten a strike by then, reel it in and make another cast," he says. "To be effective you must fish the lure very slowly. Just remember than the bass are sluggish this time of the year. A lot of your strikes will come when the lure is sitting still."

Martin will not normally use a worm or plastic lizard until the water temperature reaches 60 degrees or above, except in South Florida where a worm seems to work regardless of water temperature. He uses 4-, 5- and 6-inch plastic worms, eels and lizards for most of his spring worm fishing.

"In the spring I fish fairly light slip sinkers, 1/8 ounce to 3/16 ounce," he says. "The only time I use a heavier sinker is when I'm fishing real heavy cover and I need the additional weight to get through the cover. When fishing a worm this time of the year, when the water is still cold, I drag it very slowly,"

A mid-day rise in water temperature and shallow water activity may denote the transition to spring patterns. Spinnerbaits and buzzbaits are top lure choices then.

A good rule of thumb, according to the Texas pro, is to fish worms very slowly until the water temperature reaches 70 degrees. Then you can start fishing the worms faster while still keeping contact with the bottom. Martin will 'hop' his worm once the water warms up.

At this tough time of year, special tactics may help put more bass in the boat. Productive patterns are often difficult to come by during the transition each year. Finding one or two is a great way to enjoy the warming rays of spring.

CHAPTER 15

DELIVERANCE FROM THE DOLDRUMS

Techniques For Inactive, Structure-less Bass

THE MOST DIFFICULT fish to pattern are usually those that are either suspended away from structure or those that are simply inactive. Both situations have remedies that work sometimes.

Since more fish are inactive at any one period of time, lures that move slower should generate more strikes. It's a good idea to work a bait slowly until fish are contacted, and then either increase the speed or change to a faster lure. In this way, you are fishing for all fish, regardless of activity state, and can 'pick up' the pace after a catch to determine if an active concentration has been found.

During a major solunar period when feeding may be underway by many bass, then faster lures will cover more ground and draw strikes from the excitable foragers. Afterwards, slow down the retrieve again to appeal to inactive fish also. When bass are not concentrated, slower is better - for the stringer, and for heavy-weights.

No one loves to toss a crankbait more than I. My tackle boxes are full of them and they've all been wet. But a majority of my fish have been fooled by a worm. Like it or not, the plastic wiggler is more productive than other baits over a year's period. The reason? Action, scent and softness contribute, plus it is in front of a bass longer than most other baits. The predator has time to develop a response to the lure.

Top water plugs fished extremely slow can entice inactive fish. We have all worked on stubborn bass with the twitch-and-let-sit retrieve. It'll produce, but for best results save the surface skimmers for active times or active fish. When the lake seems to 'come alive'

Texas-rigged worms with the addition of an attractant can find action when drifted along the bottom of an old reservoir. They often attract "structure-less bass.

with the sounds of random splashing in and around the cover, or even in the middle, bass are feeding. At such times, they are not at all reticent to strike a lure on top.

Artificial top water baits attract those predators that seem intent on busting the lure into a million pieces. The bass are excited. It doesn't take a genius to pattern them. They're 'activated' for foraging. The presence of the lure and its trying to get away motivates the bass.

Flippin' is an extremely effective technique for pulling bass from heavy cover. It takes a mental adjustment by the angler, however, to be successful at it. It evolves around a much slower pace than 'run-and-gun' spinner baiting. An intense, extremely observant, yet laid-back attitude is usually best suited for this technique.

The fish in such heavy cover are inactive, and it sometimes takes patience to provoke one to strike. It's a slow way to cover a lot of ground, but a concentration of inactive fish spread throughout dense weedbeds or submerged bushes may be more worthwhile than an elusive migration of feeding bass.

Structure-less Bass

New impoundments with an abundance of submerged cover usually provide great fishery. The habitat is enormous, like that found in many natural lakes, and so can be the bass fishing. But reservoirs and other man-constructed waterways do age. They lose their vitality, chiefly the forage-intensive structures, and as a result, fishing becomes more difficult for the average bass angler.

There are reasons why fisheries in the older impoundments suffer, and there are reasons why some fishermen continue to catch bass from the "structure-less" waters. Newly-flooded reservoirs with a varying topography usually have an abundance of habitat consisting of live trees and vegetation. The tremendous cover causes an explosion of the fishery.

After a few years, usually four or five, the bass fishing peaks. Numerous three and four pounders are seemingly everywhere throughout the shallows. The bass population is slowly affected by loss of the foliage and brush, and by increasing fishing pressure. Most trees begin to rot and decompose after a few years, falling to the bottom and deteriorating to silt. The once impenetrable flooded forest is left with a few large tree trunks emerging from the water.

The fishery begins to suffer and the visible-structure hunters have less to find. As habitat disappears, micro-organisms and plankton growth diminishes. Decaying vegetation in an older impoundment has a critical influence on pH in the immediate area. Such decay is very acidic and can drive fish away if the pH value becomes too low. Additionally, while not as important as pH, oxygen in those waters is consumed by the decaying matter. No longer is the vegetation alive and generating oxygen.

Along with the disappearance of plankton and micro-organisms, a dwindling of the forage base that feeds on such tiny items occurs. The entire food chain is affected when the predator bass can't find enough crayfish, shiners or shad to satisfy his appetite. Continued population and individual growth becomes difficult.

While the numbers of bass may not be what it once was, there are usually still plenty around to catch. They are not concentrated any longer in the dense, shallow cover that was once present. The tree tops, brush, weedbeds, etc. may be long gone, so a successful angler must check out areas for other things. He must adapt to a seemingly "structure-less" environment, just like the existing bass has done.

The Structural Substitutes

Bass have two forms of safety that they can rely on. The obvious one to all anglers is cover, or as it is often known, "structure". When that is not available, then depth and elevation changes suffice for habitat. In old man-made impoundments, such as strip pits, barrow pits, etc., a lack of structure is often the rule.

Finding a brush pile on a sharp dropoff, unless recently placed there, may be extremely difficult. Even if the brush is gone, however, the topographical variations still exist in most reservoirs.

A few of these waters aren't so lucky; they lose habitat and bottom "character". In some old reservoirs, silt may build up and take its toll by covering the ditches, roadbeds, points and other drops along the bottom.

In one phosphate pit with which I'm familiar, the inflow of sludge had the effect of filling all cavities and depressions along a variable bottom. With the influx of the thick silt piped in from another pit being drained, the valleys filled to inundate the peaks. The drops off the sides of humps in 25 feet of water (down to 45 feet of water) simply disappeared. The lake floor became a very flat 25 feet in depth.

Such waters are rare, fortunately, and even huge draglines that excavate pits for various purposes leave uneven bottoms. Rock formations and other tough material make it difficult for a dragline operator to dig up a uniform amount of earth. Therefore, they don't often leave the barren lake beds that most fishery managers and knowledgeable anglers dislike.

Another "structural substitute" is found in open water, in the form of nomadic schools of forage. Threadfin shad, for example,

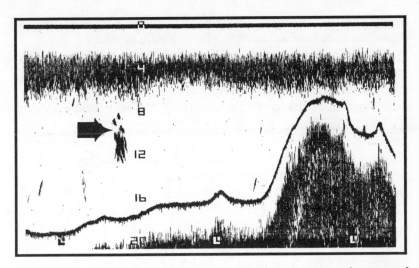

FIGURE 22 - When an impoundment loses most of its structure over the course of many years, bass relocate to deeper water for safety and protection. They may be suspended and not holding on topographical variations. That makes them difficult to catch. Drifting or trolling live or artificial baits at the right depth is normally required to be successful on "structure-less" waters.

roam the deep waters of an older reservoir and influence the location of bass. While the largemouth is primarily an ambush-type forager, he is adept at chasing down schools of shad. Often, finding a school of bass trying to herd threadfin to the surface in a foraging foray may be the best way to contact a concentration of the predator.

In the "structure-less" impoundments and pits, meandering schools of forage take on a new prominence in the life style of the existing bass. Predator movements are then more related to the location of their prey. Schooling action on such waters usually increases as shallow water structures disappear. The wise angler will be able to adjust to the movement variations.

Tactical Changes

The "up close and personal" crowd will have to change their techniques to catch bass in the older impoundments. Flippin' the shallow visible cover is now out; trolling or drifting away from the shoreline is in. Covering a lot of water is usually advisable, as bass are often less concentrated in waters having little structure.

In such an environment, even small depressions can attract bass. In fact, the very minor changes in topography take on a new significance with respect to the survival of a fishery. Many of the slight depth variations that could be important to a drift fisherman may even be difficult to detect on all but the most sophisticated sonar units.

Rod sensitivity becomes vital when fishing the depths. Line length off the spool and, correspondingly, line stretch is greater, and that dampens the strike. Detection becomes more difficult with high-stretch line and a light-action fiberglass rod. My gear consists of Berkley Series One, 100% graphite rods, and level wind reels spooled with TriMax Photochromic line. I like the 6 1/2 and 7 foot, medium heavy action versions for either drifting or trolling. In areas with little structure and visibility of two to three feet, I'll opt for 12 pound test. In super clear waters, I may use as light as 8 pound test TriMax.

Man-Made Lakes

It may be difficult to understand why an angler can catch several bass from the middle of a lake with very little cover or discernible bottom variation. I was impressed when I drifted with Texas-rigged plastic worms down the middle of an "activity" lake that was well beyond its prime. The shallow shores were crowded with swimmers and the near-shore activity was bustling with water skiers and jet skiers most everywhere I looked.

Two friends had lured me to the popular lake with promises of 15 or 20 largemouth each. The two-foot-deep crystal clear waters gradually deepened 50 feet from shore before dropping off, so I had my doubts. After seeing the boat traffic, I really had doubts. Within 10 minutes of starting our drift, however, I was a converted to fishing the middle of the dishpan lake.

We all had bass strike our wigglers before drifting more than 100 yards. The fish weren't large, maybe 1 1/2 pounds, but they were hungry. After a couple of passes over barren bottom with just a "hint" of plant life on it, we had caught and released 10 largemouth.

Deep diving crankbaits are excellent fare to troll through the depths. With limited structure below, trophy-size bass can be whipped easily.

We rigged up a second rod each then and often had two bass on at the same time. The three of us finished the four hour trip with about 40 bass taken and returned to the lake.

Trolling with either the outboard or electric motor can be just as effective on lakes with minimal structure. Hang-ups are obviously less of a concern and a maximum amount of water can be covered with such methods. Use an LCD or graph to determine what topographical changes are present, and follow any bottom paths such as ridges or elevation changes.

Keeping the lure or bait near the bottom should enhance the possibility of a strike. Bass in lakes without structure in the mid-range of the water column (that water between bottom and surface), usually opt for holding near the bottom. Put a lure within a distance of no more that twice the water visibility, and the largemouth should find it.

While trolled crankbaits are especially productive, the lure or bait doesn't need to make a lot of noise coming through the water. In fact, Texas-rigged worms and wood baits are very effective when pulled behind the boat. Each, of course, sends out small vibrations as they move and that usually attracts the bass. Even artificials with seemingly little action can attract bass from "structure-less" depths.

Live bait is particularly effective when trolled through the depths. As shallow cover and forage diminish and bass retreat to deeper hangouts, they rely on their instincts to survive. They often become more careful in their foraging and movements. Their world of dense habitat and safety is gone and their reactions require a new understanding.

Live crayfish and shiners cannot be more realistic, nor can they be more enticing. I've trolled live shiners down the open water arms of reservoirs with great success. Several largemouth between 8 and 11 pounds have succumbed to the charm of an 8-inch shiner. When operating the electric slowly, I'll use a live bait without weight, and when trolling at a faster speed, I'll add a rubber-cored sinker about 2 foot in front of the bait.

Bass can be patterned in the "structure-less" depths, and those clever enough to figure out the deep water locations of bass, and the timing, will succeed. In most waters with little shallow cover, bass can be caught away from the shore.

A reward for fishing the depths is often the biggest bass of one's life. Trophy-size largemouth, in particular, inhabit the depths and an angler drifting or trolling those areas may come across one. With little or no structure to interfere with the battle, even large fish can be effectively handled on relatively light line. The battlegrounds in such waters couldn't be more strategic, from an angler's viewpoint!

BASS SERIES LIBRARY!

Eight Great Books With A Wealth Of Information For Bass Fishermen

By Larry Larsen

I. FOLLOW THE FORAGE FOR BETTER BASS ANGLING - VOLUME 1 BASS/PREY RELATIONSHIP - The most important key to catching bass is finding them in a feeding mood. Knowing the predominant forage, its activity and availability, as well as its location in a body of water will enable an angler to catch more and larger bass. Whether you fish artificial lures or live bait, you will benefit from this book.

SPECIAL FEATURES

o PREDATOR/FORAGE INTERACTION
o BASS FEEDING BEHAVIOR
o UNDERSTANDING BASS FORAGE
o BASS/PREY PREFERENCES
o FORAGE ACTIVITY CHART

II. FOLLOW THE FORAGE FOR BETTER BASS ANGLING - VOLUME 2 TECHNIQUES - Beginners and veterans alike will achieve more success utilizing proven concepts that are based on predator/forage interactions. Understanding the reasons behind lure or bait success will result in highly productive, bass-catching patterns.

SPECIAL FEATURES

o LURE SELECTION CRITERIA
o EFFECTIVE PATTERN DEVELOPMENT
o NEW BASS CATCHING TACTICS
o FORAGING HABITAT
o BAIT AND LURE METHODS

III. BASS PRO STRATEGIES - Professional fishermen have opportunities to devote extended amounts of time to analyzing a body of water and planning a productive day on it. They know how changes in pH, water temperature, color and fluctuations affect bass fishing, and they know how to adapt to weather and topographical variations. This book reveals the methods that the country's most successful tournament anglers have employed to catch bass almost every time out. The reader's productivity should improve after spending a few hours with this compilation of techniques!

SPECIAL FEATURES

o MAPPING & WATER ELIMINATION
o LOCATE DEEP & SHALLOW BASS
o BOAT POSITION FACTORS
o WATER CHEMISTRY INFLUENCES
o WEATHER EFFECTS
o TOPOGRAPHICAL TECHNIQUES

IV. BASS LURES - TRICKS & TECHNIQUES - Modifications of lures and development of new baits and techniques continue to keep the fare fresh, and that's important. Bass seem to become "accustomed" to the same artificials and presentations seen over and over again. As a result, they become harder to catch. It's the new approach that again sparks the interest of some largemouth. To that end, this book explores some of the latest ideas for modifying, rigging and using them. The lure modifications, tricks and techniques presented within these covers will work anywhere in the country.

SPECIAL FEATURES

o UNIQUE LURE MODIFICATIONS
o IN-DEPTH VARIABLE REASONING
o PRODUCTIVE PRESENTATIONS
o EFFECTIVE NEW RIGGINGS
o TECHNOLOGICAL ADVANCES

V. SHALLOW WATER BASS - Catching shallow water large-mouth is not particularly difficult. Catching lots of them usually is. Even more challenging is catching lunker-size bass in seasons other than during the spring spawn. Anglers applying the information within the covers of this book on marshes, estuaries, reservoirs, lakes, creeks or small ponds should triple their results. The book details productive new tactics to apply to thin-water angling. Numerous photographs and figures easily define the optimal locations and proven methods to catch bass.

SPECIAL FEATURES

o UNDERSTANDING BASS/COVER INTERFACE
o METHODS TO LOCATE BASS CONCENTRATIONS
o ANALYSIS OF WATER TYPES
o TACTICS FOR SPECIFIC HABITATS
o LARSEN'S "FLORA FACTOR"

VI. BASS FISHING FACTS - This angler's guide to the lifestyles and behavior of the black bass is a reference source of sorts, never before compiled. The book explores the behavior of bass during pre- and post-spawn as well as during bedding season. It examines how bass utilize their senses to feed and how they respond to environmental factors. The book details how fishermen can be more productive by applying such knowledge to their bass angling. The information within the covers of this book includes those bass species, known as "other" bass, such as redeye, Suwannee, spotted, etc.

SPECIAL FEATURES

o BASS FORAGING MOTIVATORS
o DETAILED SPRING MOVEMENTS
o A LOOK AT BASS SENSES
o GENETIC INTRODUCTION/STUDIES
o MINOR BASS SPECIES & HABITATS

VII. TROPHY BASS - is focused at today's dedicated lunker hunters who find more enjoyment in wrestling with one or two monster largemouth than with a "panfull" of yearlings. To help the reader better understand how to catch big bass, a majority of this book explores productive techniques for trophies. The "how to" information was gleaned from professional guides and other experienced trophy bass hunters. This book takes a look at the geographical areas and waters that offer better opportunities to catch giant bass.

SPECIAL FEATURES

o GEOGRAPHIC DISTRIBUTIONS
o STATE RECORD INFORMATION
o GENETIC GIANTS
o TECHNIQUES FOR TROPHIES
o LOCATION CONSIDERATIONS
o LURE AND BAIT TIMING

VIII. AN ANGLER'S GUIDE TO BASS PATTERNS examines the most effective combination of lure, method and places. Being able to develop a pattern of successful methods and lures for specific habitats and environmental conditions is the key to catching several bass on each fishing trip. Understanding bass movements and activities and the most appropriate and effective techniques to employ will add many pounds of enjoyment to the sport of bass fishing. "Bass Patterns" is a reference source for all anglers, regardless of where they live or their skill level.

SPECIAL FEATURES

o BOAT POSITIONING
o NEW WATER STRATEGIES
o DEPTH AND COVER CONCEPTS
o MOVING WATER TACTICS
o WEATHER/ACTIVITY FACTORS
o TRANSITIONAL TECHNIQUES

LARSEN'S OUTDOOR PUBLISHING

CONVENIENT ORDER FORM

Please send me the following book(s):

———— I. BETTER BASS ANGLING - VOLUME 1 BASS/PREY
           INTERACTION
———— II. BETTER BASS ANGLING - VOLUME 2 TECHNIQUES
———— III. BASS PRO STRATEGIES
———— IV. BASS LURES - TRICKS & TECHNIQUES
———— V. SHALLOW WATER BASS
———— VI. BASS FISHING FACTS
———— VII. TROPHY BASS
———— VIII. ANGLER'S GUIDE TO BASS PATTERNS

Priced at $11.95 each which includes postage and handling.

Discount 10% if ordering two or three books. Discount 20% if ordering four or more books. Order the entire "Bass Series Library" of eight personally-autographed books for a total price of only $69.95, which includes handling and postage. Please allow three weeks for delivery. Thanks.

NAME_____

ADDRESS_____

CITY_____STATE_____ZIP_____

Number of books being ordered = _____ x $11.95

TOTAL AMOUNT ENCLOSED (Check or Money Order) $_____

Copy this page and mail to:
Larry Larsen
Larsen's Outdoor Publishing
Dept. "BK78"
2640 Elizabeth Place
Lakeland, FL 33813

LARSEN'S OUTDOOR PUBLISHING

CONVENIENT ORDER FORM

Please send me the following book(s):

—— I. BETTER BASS ANGLING - VOLUME 1 BASS/PREY
   INTERACTION
—— II. BETTER BASS ANGLING - VOLUME 2 TECHNIQUES
—— III. BASS PRO STRATEGIES
—— IV. BASS LURES - TRICKS & TECHNIQUES
—— V. SHALLOW WATER BASS
—— VI. BASS FISHING FACTS
—— VII. TROPHY BASS
—— VIII. ANGLER'S GUIDE TO BASS PATTERNS

Priced at $11.95 each which includes postage and handling.

Discount 10% if ordering two or three books. Discount 20% if ordering four or more books. Order the entire "Bass Series Library" of eight personally-autographed books for a total price of only $69.95, which includes handling and postage. Please allow three weeks for delivery. Thanks.

NAME_____

ADDRESS_____

CITY_____STATE_____ZIP_____

Number of books being ordered = _____ x $11.95

TOTAL AMOUNT ENCLOSED (Check or Money Order) $_____

Copy this page and mail to:
Larry Larsen
Larsen's Outdoor Publishing
Dept. "BK78"
2640 Elizabeth Place
Lakeland, FL 33813